BULLETIN BOARDS TO TEACH THE BIBLE

by
SUSAN JULIO

illustrated by Becky Radtke

Cover by Ted Warren

Copyright © 1994, Shining Star Publications

ISBN No. 1-56417-003-9

Standardized Subject Code TA ac

Printing No. 9876

Shining Star
A Division of Frank Schaffer Publications, Inc.
23740 Hawthorne Boulevard
Torrance, CA 90505-5927

Unless otherwise indicated, the New International Version of the Bible was used in preparing the activities in this book.

TO THE TEACHER/PARENT

This book is filled with Bible-based bulletin board ideas that relate to both Old and New Testament themes. Holiday bulletin board ideas are included as well, which makes this book useful throughout the year.

Each bulletin board is designed to enable your students to become active learners. The students actually perform tasks that reinforce what is being taught. Sometimes students must refer to the Bible, a concordance, or another reference book. The boards may be used just for fun, or you can set up a reward system. If you use a reward system, assign points to each board used. When students complete the activity, the points earned are used for extra credit or a special treat. Although Bible verse references are sometimes provided, you may choose to leave the references off when reproducing the board. This will present a greater challenge for your students.

The bulletin board patterns may be enlarged, or left as is, depending on the amount of space you have. A simple way of enlarging a pattern is to trace it on a sheet of acetate. Tape an appropriately sized piece of paper on the wall and use an overhead projector to shine the image onto the piece of paper. The image may be made larger or smaller by moving the projector farther or nearer to the wall. When the image is the right size, trace it on the paper.

I suggest that you introduce each bulletin board to your class by discussing its theme. Give instructions on how to use the board correctly. In order to make the bulletin board pieces last longer, you may want to mount them on tagboard and laminate them. When you use Velcro™ pieces, show your students the correct way to remove them from the board. Place one hand on the board and slowly peel off the pieces. Removable pieces should be kept in plastic Ziploc™ Storage Bags that are attached with pushpins to the bottom of the board. Since some of the boards require students to look up verses in the Bible, provide instructions on finding Scripture references.

I hope that *Bulletin Boards to Teach the Bible* will brighten your classroom as well as challenge and motivate your students to learn more about God's Word!

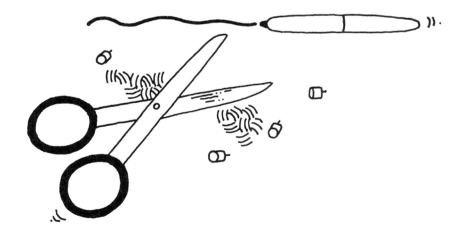

TABLE OF CONTENTS

DEDICATION

To my mother, Catherine Wloszek, with love.

SS3825

NOAH'S ARK

(raindrop labels:)
1. 1 Peter 5:8
2. 1 Samuel 17:43
3. Song of Songs 2:15
4. Mark 5:1-13
5. Acts 28:3-5
6. 1 Kings 10:21-22
7. Deuteronomy 1:44
8. Matthew 23:37
9. Proverbs 30:25
10. Exodus 8:2-15

Directions
Did you know that you can find many different kinds of animals in the Bible? Help Noah fill his ark by looking up the Bible verse on each raindrop and finding the name of an animal. Write your answers on a piece of paper. When you are done, take Noah out of the ark and check your answers.

Materials:

gray background, construction paper (all colors), scissors, stapler, markers (including black), paper, pencil

Directions:

1. Cover the board with the background paper and cut letters for the caption from rainbow colors of construction paper.
2. Reproduce and enlarge the ark on page 6. Trace it on brown construction paper and cut it out. Write these directions on the ark: Did you know that you can find many different kinds of animals in the Bible? Help Noah fill his ark by looking up the Bible verse on each raindrop and finding the name of an animal. Write your answers on a piece of paper. When you are done, take Noah out of the ark and check your answers.
3. Staple the ark to the board, leaving a space to slide in Noah.
4. Reproduce, color, and cut out Noah from the pattern on page 6.
5. Reproduce the raindrop pattern on page 6. Trace ten raindrops on blue construction paper and cut them out. On each drop, write one of the following numbers and verses:
   1. 1 Peter 5:8
   2. 1 Samuel 17:43
   3. Song of Songs 2:15
   4. Mark 5:1-13
   5. Acts 28:3-5
   6. 1 Kings 10:21-22
   7. Deuteronomy 1:44
   8. Matthew 23:37
   9. Proverbs 30:25
   10. Exodus 8:2-15

   Attach the drops to the board.

Follow-Up:

Have each student draw and cut out a picture of a favorite animal. Slide it into the ark along with Noah.

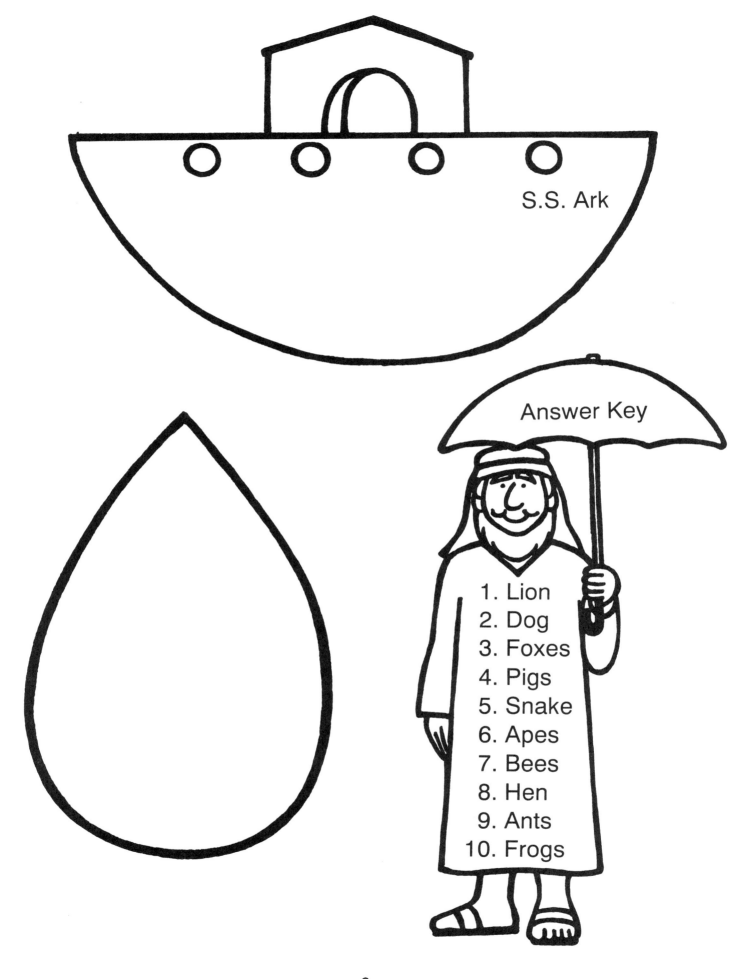

S.S. Ark

Answer Key

1. Lion
2. Dog
3. Foxes
4. Pigs
5. Snake
6. Apes
7. Bees
8. Hen
9. Ants
10. Frogs

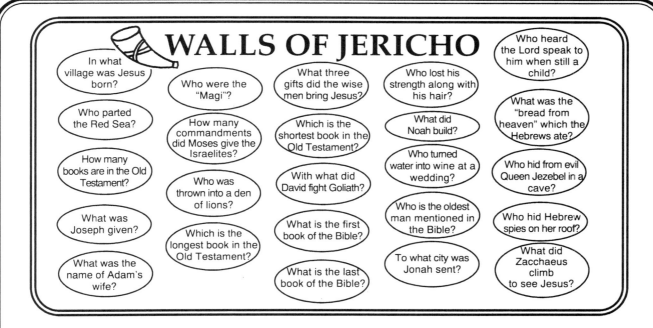

Materials:

brown background paper, black marker, construction paper (green, gray, yellow), scissors, small container, stapler, paper, pencil

Directions:

1. Cover the board with the background paper. Cut letters for the caption from green construction paper.
2. Reproduce the stone pattern on page 9. Trace and cut out twenty-four stones from gray construction paper. Print one of the following questions on each stone. (Answers are in parentheses.)
   - In what village was Jesus born? (Bethlehem–Matthew 2:1)
   - Who parted the Red Sea? (Moses–Exodus 14:21)
   - How many books are in the Old Testament? (39)
   - What was Joseph given? (A robe–Genesis 37:3)
   - What was the name of Adam's wife? (Eve–Genesis 3:20)
   - How many commandments did Moses give the Israelites? (Ten–Exodus 20)
   - Who were the "Magi"? (Wise men–Matthew 2)
   - Who was thrown into a den of lions? (Daniel–Daniel 6:16)
   - What did Noah build? (An ark–Genesis 6:14)
   - Which is the longest book in the Old Testament? (Psalms)
   - Which is the shortest book in the Old Testament? (Obadiah)
   - With what did David fight Goliath? (A sling and a stone– 1 Samuel 17:49-50)
   - What is the first book of the Bible? (Genesis)
   - What is the last book of the Bible? (Revelation)
   - Who lost his strength along with his hair? (Samson–Judges 16:19-20)
   - What three gifts did the wise men bring Jesus? (Gold, incense, myrrh–Matthew 2:11)
   - Who turned water into wine at a wedding? (Jesus–John 2)
   - Who is the oldest man mentioned in the Bible? (Methuselah–Genesis 5:27)
   - To what city was Jonah sent? (Nineveh–Jonah 1:2)

SS3825

- Who heard the Lord speak to him when still a child? (Samuel–1 Samuel 3)
- What was the "bread from heaven" which the Hebrews ate? (Manna–Exodus 16:31)
- Who hid from evil Queen Jezebel in a cave? (Elijah–1 Kings 19)
- What did Zacchaeus climb to see Jesus? (A sycamore-fig tree–Luke 19:1-4)
- Who hid Hebrew spies on her roof? (Rahab–Joshua 2:1-6)

3. Attach the stones to the board as shown.
4. Reproduce the trumpet pattern on page 9. Trace a trumpet from yellow construction paper.
5. Review the story of Joshua and Jericho with the class. Announce that there is going to be a contest to see how long it takes for the walls of Jericho to come down a second time. Call attention to the bulletin board and the question stones. Every morning when students come in, they will see the paper trumpet tucked behind one particular stone. At some point during the day, each student should write on a small slip of paper the answer to the question on that stone. The paper should be put in a container on the teacher's desk. At the end of the day, the teacher will pull out an answer. If it's correct, the student who wrote it will remove that stone from the wall. This procedure is repeated until all the stones are removed.

Follow-Up:

For a year-round extension of this activity, cover a shoe box with paper and construction paper question marks. Cut a slit in the lid of the box. Encourage students to write their own Bible questions (and answers) on slips of paper and put them in the box. During "free moments" draw a question for the class to answer.

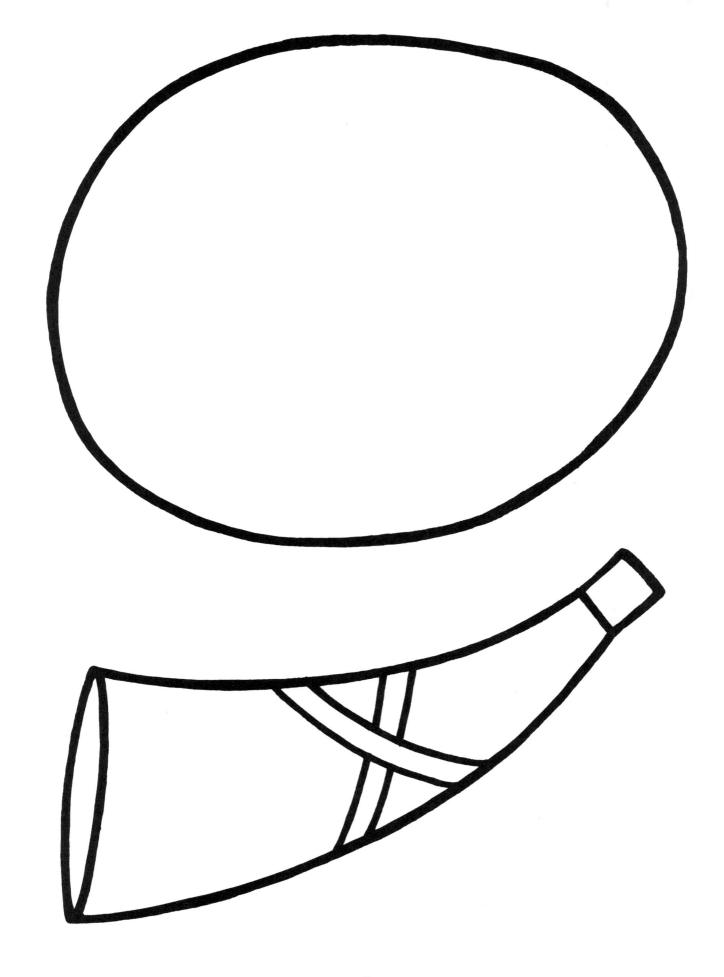

SS3825

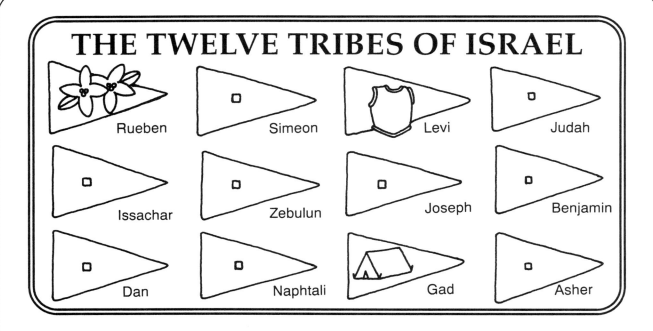

THE TWELVE TRIBES OF ISRAEL

Rueben   Simeon   Levi   Judah

Issachar   Zebulun   Joseph   Benjamin

Dan   Naphtali   Gad   Asher

Materials:

white background paper, construction paper (all colors), stapler, Velcro™ strips, scissors, markers (including black), 5" x 9" card, large plastic storage bag, pencil, pushpins

Directions:

1. Cover the board with the background paper. Cut letters for the caption from black construction paper.
2. Reproduce the banner on page 11. Trace and cut twelve banners from different colors of construction paper. Attach them to the board as shown. Apply a small piece of Velcro™ to the center of each banner. Using a black marker, write the name of a tribe under each one.
3. Reproduce, color, and cut out the tribe symbols on pages 12-17. Attach Velcro™ to the back of each.
4. Print the following directions on a 5" x 9" card:
   The twelve tribes of Israel are the descendents of Jacob's twelve sons: Rueben, Simeon, Levi, Judah, Issachar, Zebulun, Joseph, Benjamin, Dan, Naphtali, Gad, and Asher. Each of the twelve tribes was given a special place to live in the Promised Land. Tradition says each was given a special symbol that stood for the tribal name. See if you can match these special symbols with the tribal banners. Hint: Read Genesis 49 for some clues! (Look on the back of the card to check your work when you are done.)
   On the back of the card write this answer key:
   Reuben–Mandrake Plant, Simeon–City Gate, Levi–Breastplate, Judah–Lion, Issachar–Donkey, Zebulun–Ship, Joseph–Grain, Benjamin–Wolf, Dan–Serpent, Naphtali–Doe, Gad–Tent, Asher–Olive Tree
5. Store the directions card and tribe symbols in a storage bag, and secure it to the board with pushpins.

Follow-Up:

Have each student design a banner and symbol for his own "tribe" (family). Let them share their banners with the class.

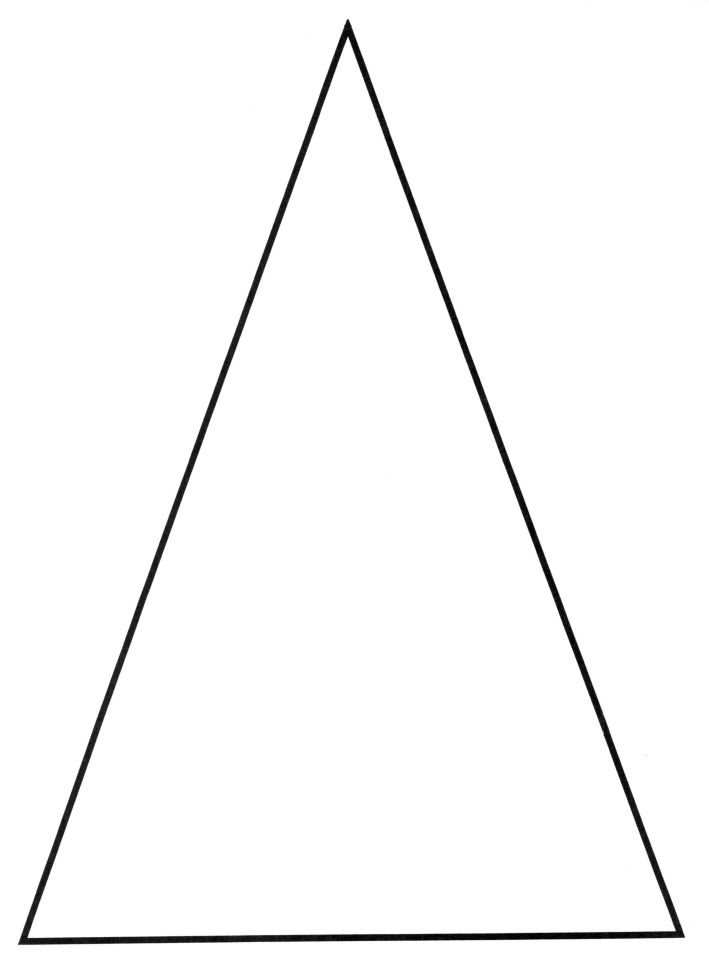

SS3825

Donkey

Ship

SS3825

Tent

Olive Tree

SS3825

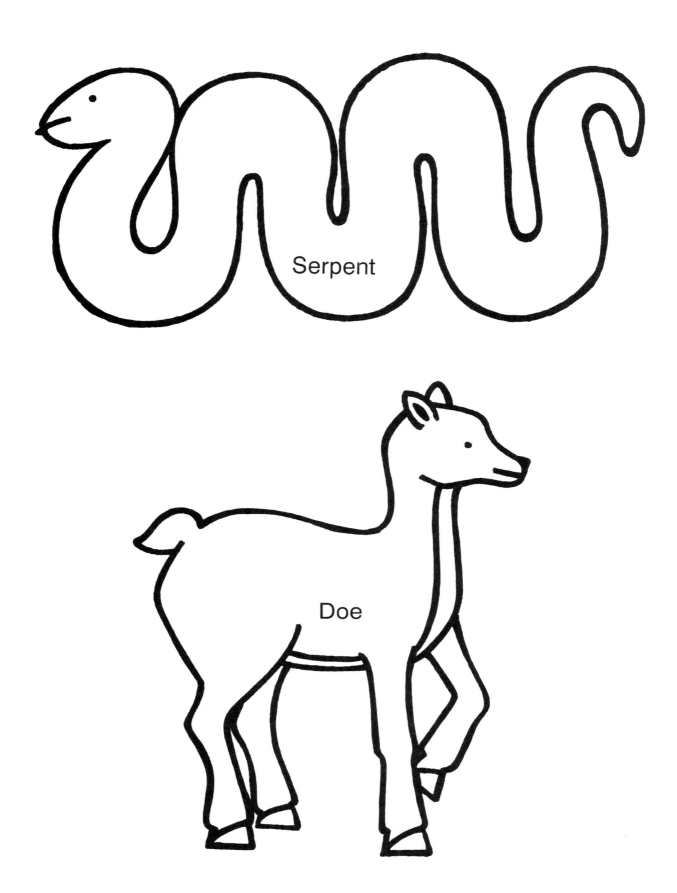

Serpent

Doe

SS3825

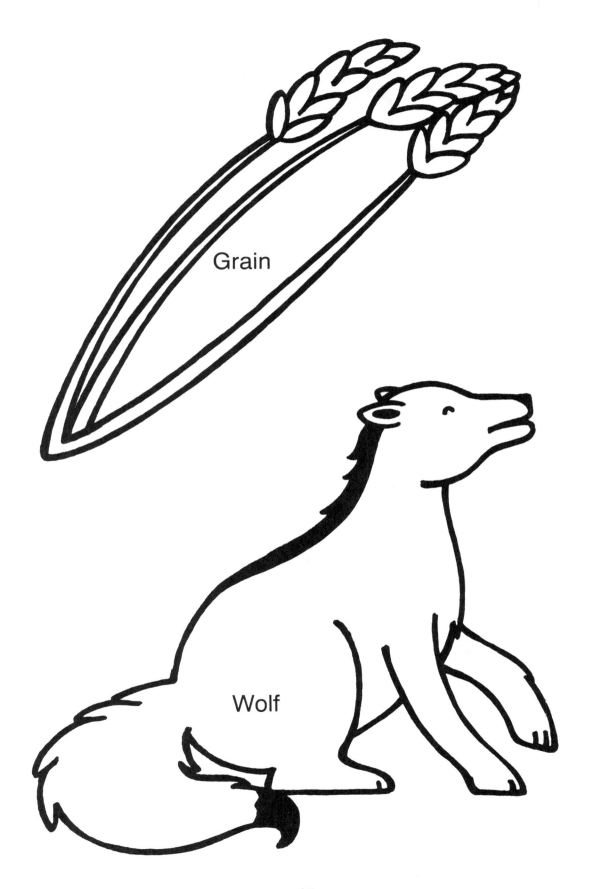

Grain

Wolf

SS3825

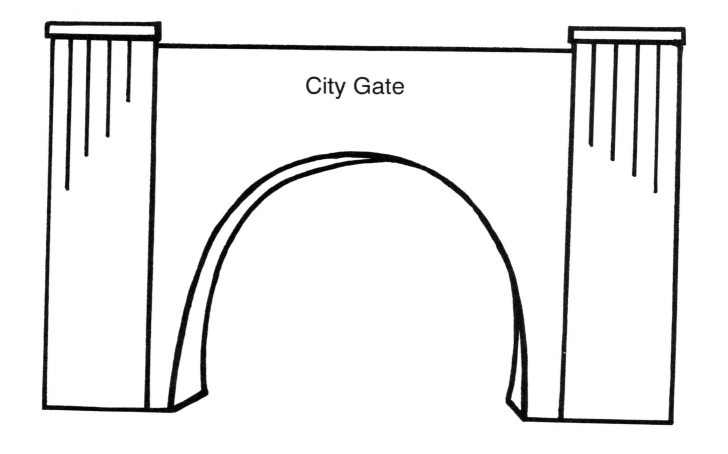

City Gate

Mandrake Plant

SS3825

Breastplate

Lion

17

Materials:

background paper (a light color), markers (including black), stapler, scissors, pushpins, construction paper (black, yellow), pencil, paper

Directions:

1. Cover the board with background paper and cut letters for the caption from black construction paper.
2. Reproduce, color, and cut out the prophet pictures on pages 19-21. Staple them to the board.
3. Reproduce, trace, and cut the key on page 21 from yellow construction paper. On the front of the key, write these directions:
   The Old Testament is filled with exciting stories about the prophets—men called by God to tell about future events. Read each picture and, using your Bible, see if you can guess "Who Am I?" Write your answers on a piece of paper. (Check your answers by turning this key over when you are done.)
   On the back of the key write these answers:
   1. Elijah   2. Daniel   3. Jonah   4. Ezekiel   5. Elisha
4. Attach the key to the board with a pushpin.

Follow-Up:

When you are ready to take the board down, make a copy of the prophet pictures for each student. Have them color and assemble the pictures into a "Prophet—Who Am I?" riddle book to share with friends and family.

SS3825

5
I healed a soldier of
leprosy. Who am I?
(2 Kings 5)

3
I was swallowed by a
great fish. Who am I?
(Jonah 1:17)

2
I was thrown into a
lions' den. Who am I?
(Daniel 6:16)

1
I was taken up to heaven in
a chariot of fire. Who am I?
(2 Kings 2:11)

SS3825

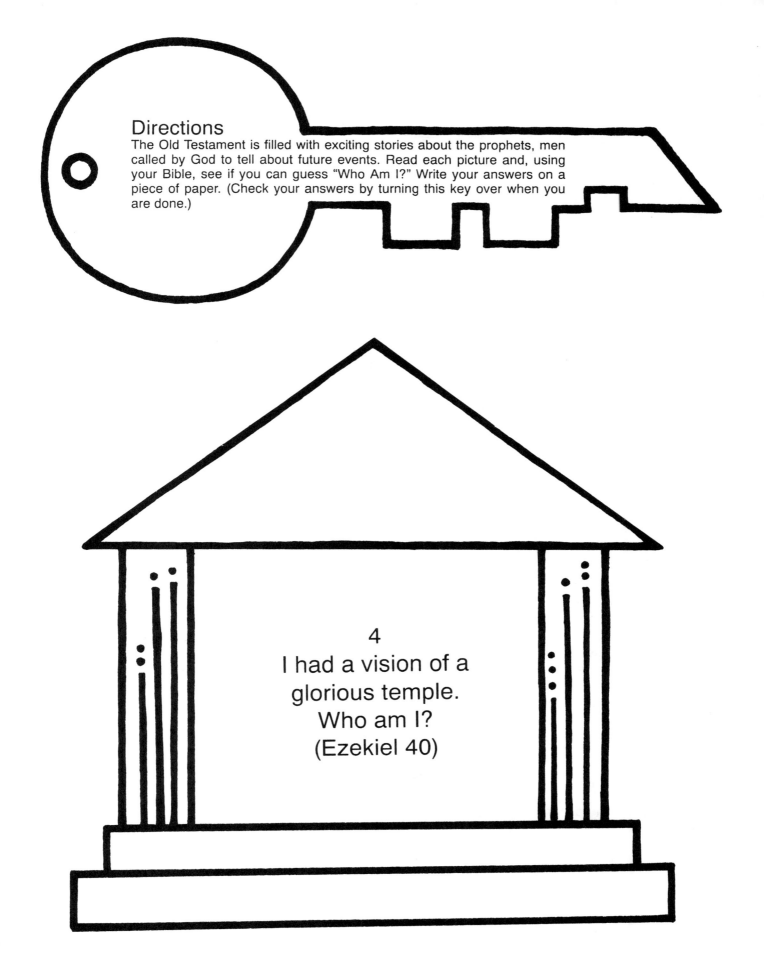

Directions

The Old Testament is filled with exciting stories about the prophets, men called by God to tell about future events. Read each picture and, using your Bible, see if you can guess "Who Am I?" Write your answers on a piece of paper. (Check your answers by turning this key over when you are done.)

4
I had a vision of a
glorious temple.
Who am I?
(Ezekiel 40)

SS3825

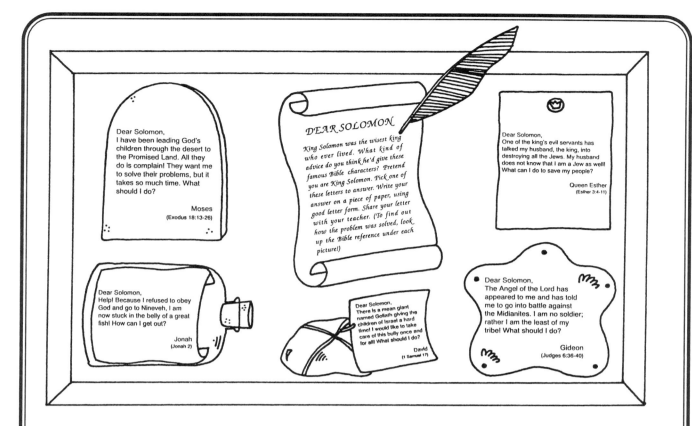

Materials:

background paper (any color), 12" x 18" piece of white construction paper, markers (including black), strip of brown construction paper, scissors, stapler, paper, pencil

Directions:

1. Cover the board with background paper.
2. Curl the bottom and top edges of the white construction paper. Use a black marker to write "Dear Solomon" at the top in large script. Print these directions underneath:
   King Solomon was the wisest king who ever lived. What kind of advice do you think he'd give these famous Bible characters? Pretend you are King Solomon. Pick one of these letters to answer. Write your answer on a piece of paper, using good letter form. Share your letter with your teacher. (To find out how the problem was solved, look up the Bible reference under each picture.)
3. Enlarge the quill pen on page 23 and trace onto brown paper. Attach it to the board.
4. Reproduce, color, and cut out each letter on pages 23-25, and staple them to the board as shown.

Follow-Up:

Post student responses on the board next to the appropriate letters.

Dear Solomon,
The Angel of the Lord has appeared to me and has told me to go into battle against the Midianites. I am no soldier; rather I am the least of my tribe! What should I do?

Gideon
(Judges 6:36-40)

SS3825

Dear Solomon,
One of the king's evil servants has talked my husband, the king, into destroying all the Jews. My husband does not know that I am a Jew as well! What can I do to save my people?

Queen Esther
(Esther 3:4-11)

Dear Solomon,
There is a mean giant named Goliath giving the children of Israel a hard time! I would like to take care of this bully once and for all! What should I do?

David
(1 Samuel 17)

SS3825

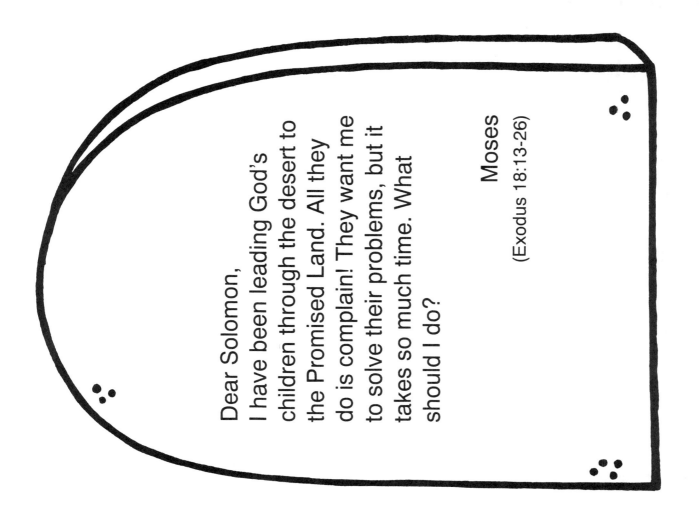

Dear Solomon,
I have been leading God's children through the desert to the Promised Land. All they do is complain! They want me to solve their problems, but it takes so much time. What should I do?

Moses
(Exodus 18:13-26)

Dear Solomon,
Help! Because I refused to obey God and go to Nineveh, I am now stuck in the belly of a great fish! How can I get out?

Jonah
(Jonah 2)

Materials:

background paper (any color), ruler, markers (including black), stapler, scissors, Velcro™ , construction paper (assorted colors), 5" x 9" index card, plastic storage bag, pencil, push-pins

Directions:

1. Cover the board with background paper. Draw two musical staffs on the board. Cut out letters for the caption from black construction paper and attach as shown.
2. Enlarge, color, and cut out the music symbols on pages 27-29. Staple them to the board. Attach a small piece of Velcro™ near each symbol.
3. Reproduce the musical notes on page 28 and trace them on five different colors of construction paper. Cut the notes out and write one of the following names on each:
   Jubal   Asaph   King Solomon   Priests   David
   Place a small piece of Velcro™ on the back of each note.
4. On the 5" x 9" card write the following directions:
   Take "note" of some famous biblical musicians by reading each of the pictures on the board. Take out the musical notes and look at the names on them. See if you can match each note with the correct picture. Use the Bible references on the pictures to help you. (When you are done, check your work by turning this card over.)
   On the back of the card write this answer key:
   1. Jubal   2. Asaph   3. King Solomon   4. Priests   5. David
5. Store the directions card and notes in the plastic bag and secure it to the board with pushpins.

Follow-Up:

Encourage students to read selections from Psalms, then come up with their own "songs" of worship. Gather together some simple instruments and tape-record children playing them.

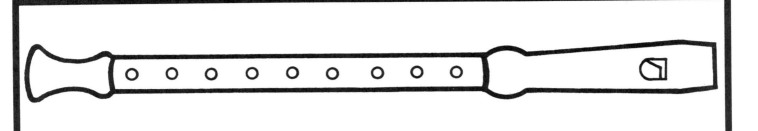

1. I invented the flute.
   (Genesis 4:21)

2. I played the cymbals before
the great ark of God.

(1 Chronicles 16:1-5)

SS3825

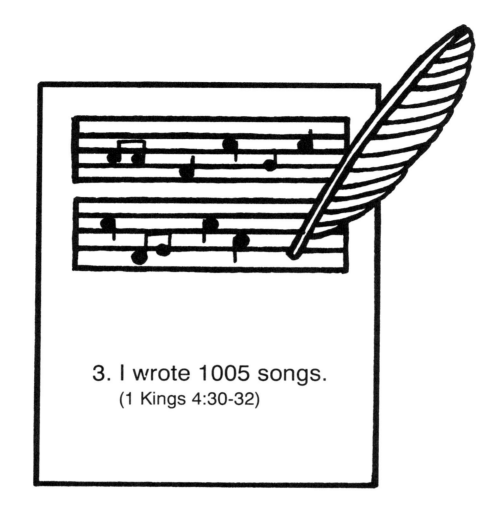

3. I wrote 1005 songs.
(1 Kings 4:30-32)

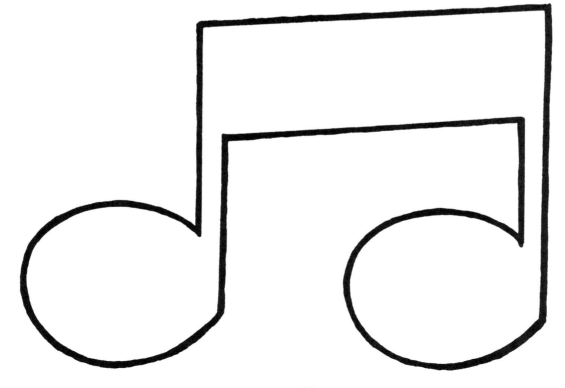

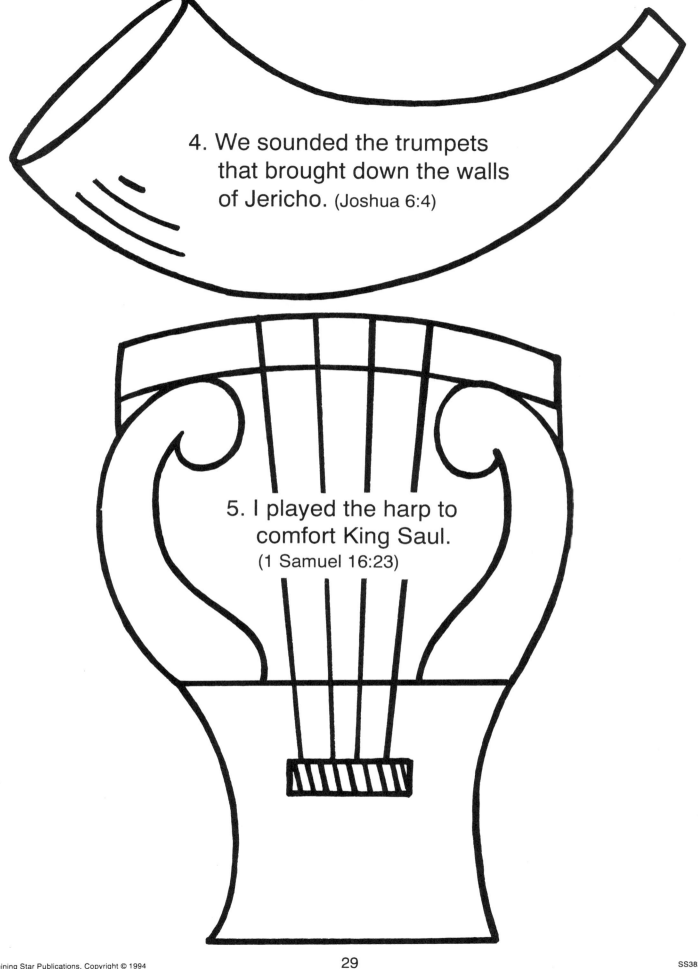

4. We sounded the trumpets that brought down the walls of Jericho. (Joshua 6:4)

5. I played the harp to comfort King Saul. (1 Samuel 16:23)

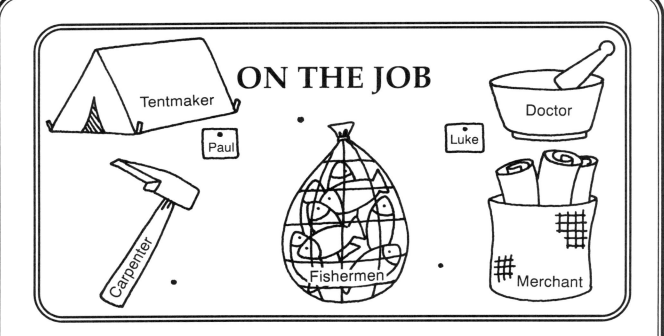

Materials:

background paper (any color), scissors, stapler, pushpins, hole punch, construction paper, crayons or markers, 5" x 9" index card, plastic storage bag

Directions:

1. Cover the board with background paper. Cut letters for the caption from construction paper.
2. Reproduce, color, and cut out the occupation symbols on pages 32-34. Attach them to the board as shown. Near each picture, place a pushpin.
3. Reproduce and cut out the business cards on page 31.
4. Write these directions on the 5" x 9" card:
   Did you know that people in the Bible had jobs, just as people do today? Each symbol on the board shows a job that a famous biblical character did. Look at each business card and, using your Bible to look up the verses, see if you can match each person with the correct occupation. (Check your answers by looking at the back of this card.)
   On the back of the card write this answer key:
   Tentmaker–Paul, Carpenter–Jesus, Merchant–Lydia, Doctor–Luke, Fishermen–Simon Peter and Andrew
5. Store the directions card and business cards in the plastic storage bag and secure it to the board.

Follow-Up:

Have students design business cards for occupations. Cards should include pictures and catchy slogans. (Example: Lydia's Purple Goods Emporium–A shade above the rest!)

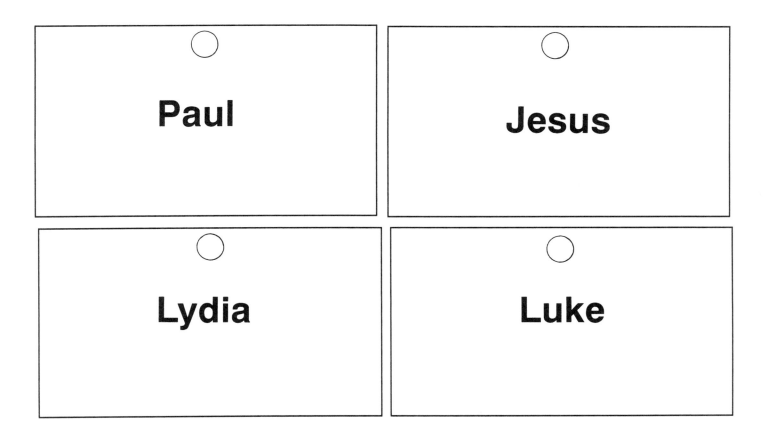

Paul

Jesus

Lydia

Luke

Simon Peter
and
Andrew

SS3825

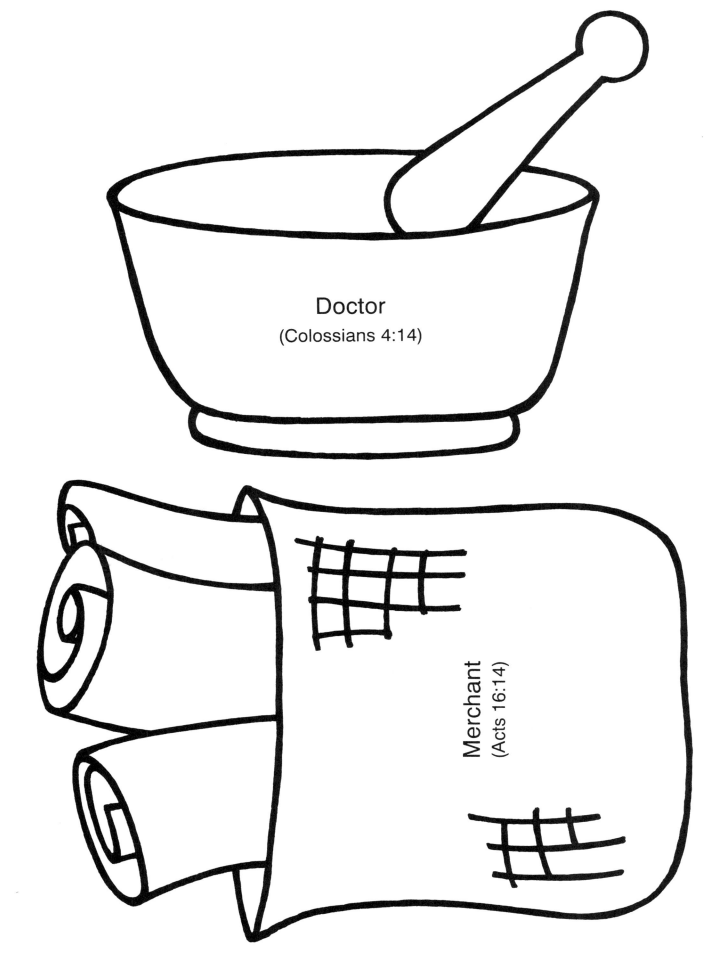

Doctor
(Colossians 4:14)

Merchant
(Acts 16:14)

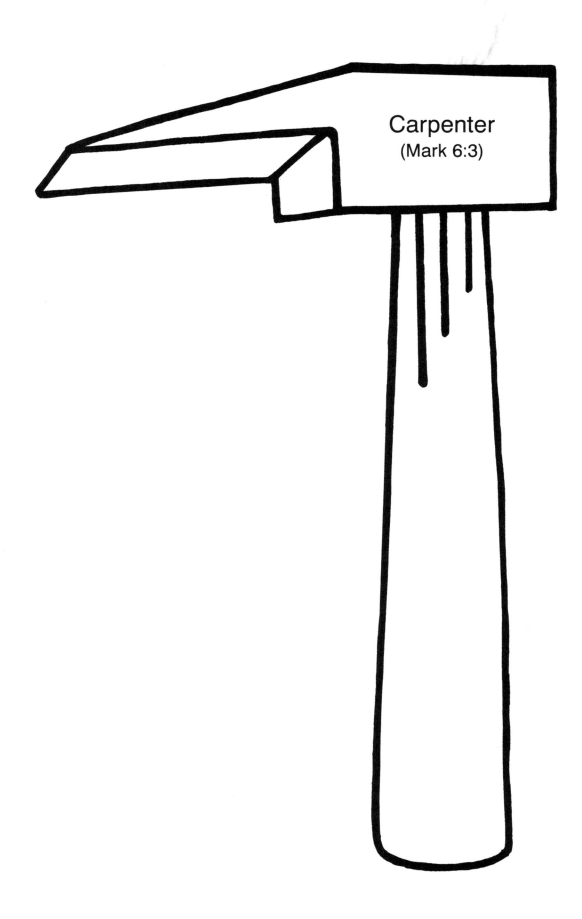

Carpenter
(Mark 6:3)

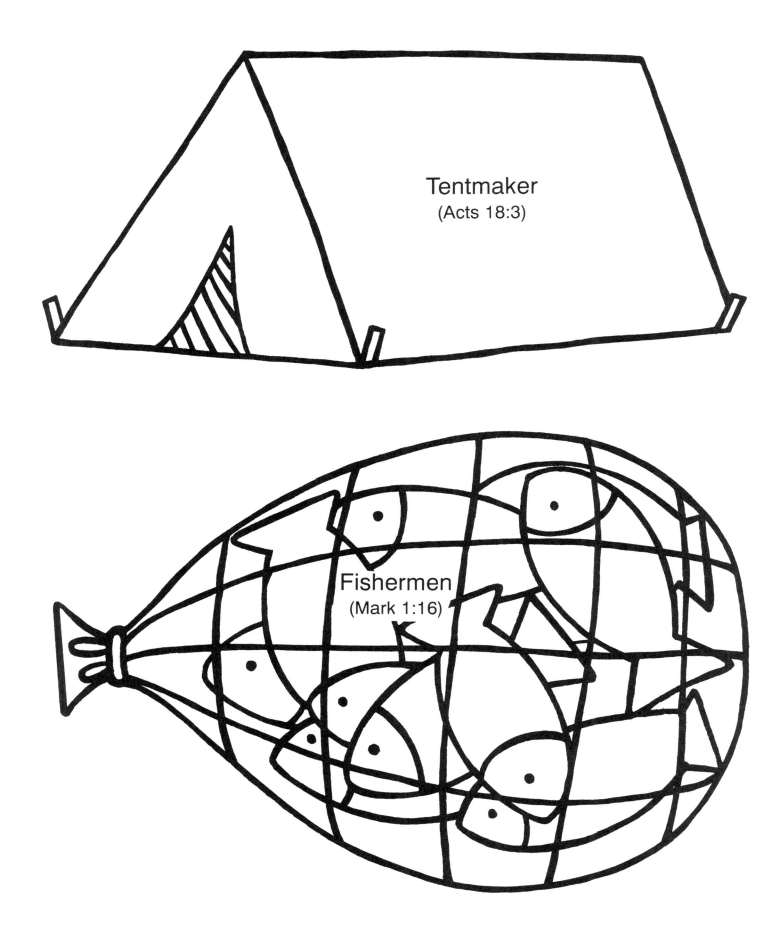

Tentmaker
(Acts 18:3)

Fishermen
(Mark 1:16)

SS3825

Bright and Morning Star   Day Spring   Lamb of God   *Word*

Judge   *Lion of Judah*   Son of God   Wonderful Counselor

Good Shepherd   **Son of Man**   King of Kings   Immanuel

Prince of Peace   **I Am**   *Lord of Lords*

NAME ABOVE ALL NAMES

 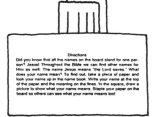 

Materials:

black background paper, colored chalk, black marker, scissors, stapler, book of names, construction paper (all colors), 5" x 9" index card

Directions:

1. Cover the board with the black background paper. Cut letters for the caption from different colors of construction paper and attach them at the center of the board. Use colored chalk to write names of Jesus: Bright and Morning Star, Lord of Lords, I Am, Judge, Word, Good Shepherd, Son of Man, Lamb of God, Prince of Peace, Anointed, Wonderful Counselor, Alpha and Omega, True Vine, Immanuel, Son of God, Lion of Judah, Day Spring, and King of Kings.

2. On the 5" x 9" card write the following directions:
   Did you know that all the names on the board stand for one person? Jesus! Throughout the Bible we can find other names for Him as well. The name Jesus means "the Lord saves." What does your name mean? To find out, take a piece of paper and look your name up in a book of names. Write your name at the top of the name slip and the meaning on the lines. In the square, draw a picture to show what your name means. Staple your paper on the board so others can see what your name means too!
   Staple the directions card to the board, leaving the top open to form a pocket.

3. Reproduce the blank name slip from page 36 and place the slips in the pocket.
   Note: When directing students' attention to the board, show them where they can find the book of names and how to use it.

Follow-Up:

Invite students to explore one of Jesus' names. When was He called by that name? What does the name mean?

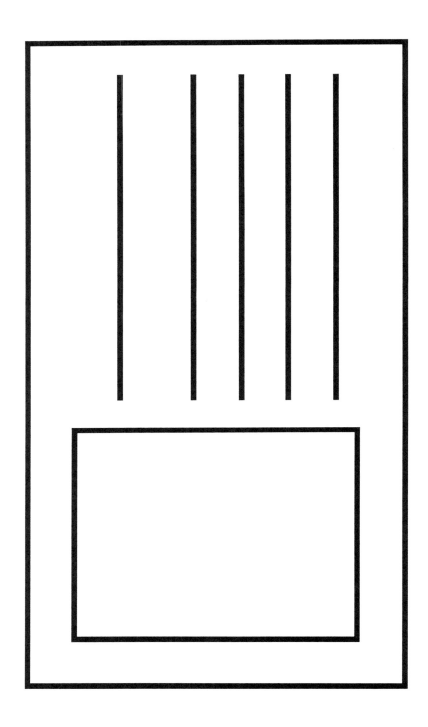

SS3825

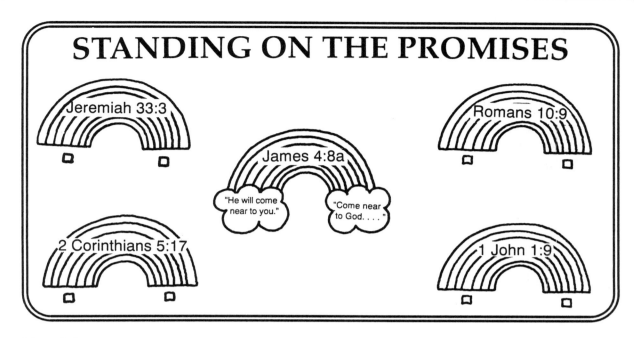

Materials:

light blue background paper, silver foil, stapler, scissors, cotton, Velcro™, white construction paper, black and red markers, colored chalk, 5" x 9" index card, plastic storage bag, pencil, pushpins

Directions:

1. Cover the board with the background paper. Cut letters for the caption from silver foil.
2. Enlarge the rainbow pattern on page 39. Trace and cut five rainbows from white paper. Color them with chalk. (Rainbow colors are red, orange, yellow, green, blue, indigo, and violet.) On each rainbow write one of the following verses in black marker:
   Romans 10:9; 1 John 1:9; 2 Corinthians 5:17; Jeremiah 33:3; James 4:8a
   Attach rainbows to the board. Place a small piece of Velcro™ under each rainbow end.
3. Reproduce the cloud pattern on page 40. Trace and cut ten clouds from white construction paper. Sort the clouds into pairs. In each pair, one cloud will be the "Promise" cloud, and the other will be the "Condition" cloud. Copy one set of Promises (use a black marker) and Conditions (use a red marker) from below:

Promises	Conditions
"You will be saved."	". . . if you confess with your mouth, 'Jesus is Lord,' and believe in your heart that God raised him from the dead."
"He is faithful and just and will forgive us our sins and purify us from all unrighteousness."	"If we confess our sins."
"He is a new creation; the old has gone, the new has come!"	". . . if anyone is in Christ."
"I will answer you and tell you great and unsearchable things you do not know."	"Call to me . . . ."
"He will come near to you."	"Come near to God . . . ."

SS3825

Glue cotton around each cloud and attach a small piece of Velcro™ to the back.

4. On the 5" x 9" card write these directions:

The Bible talks about many of the promises God gives to those who believe in Him. Sometimes a promise comes with a condition–something we must do in order to receive the promise. There are two kinds of clouds in this bag. The ones in black are the Promises; the ones in red are the Conditions. Look up the verse on each rainbow. See if you can find the promise and the condition in the verse. Put the clouds at the ends of the rainbow, Promise cloud first. (Check your answers by looking at the back of this card.)

On the back of the card write these answers:

1 John 1:9–"He is faithful and just and will forgive us our sins and purify us from all unrighteousness./If we confess our sins."

Romans 10:9–"You will be saved./. . . if you confess with your mouth, 'Jesus is Lord,' and believe in your heart that God raised him from the dead."

2 Corinthians 5:17–"He is a new creation; the old has gone, the new has come!/. . . if anyone is in Christ."

Jeremiah 33:3–"I will answer you and tell you great and unsearchable things you do not know./Call to me . . . ."

James 4:8a–"He will come near to you./ Come near to God . . . ."

5. Store directions card and clouds in a plastic storage bag and secure them to board with pushpins.

Follow-Up:

Have each student trace a foot (with or without the shoe) on construction paper. Let each select one of God's unconditional promises to write across his foot outline. (Some unconditional promises may be found in Matthew 11:30; 19:26; 28:18; Acts 10:34; Romans 14:12; 2 Timothy 2:19; Hebrews 13:8; James 1:17; 1 Peter 3:22; 2 Peter 3:9; Revelation 17:14.)

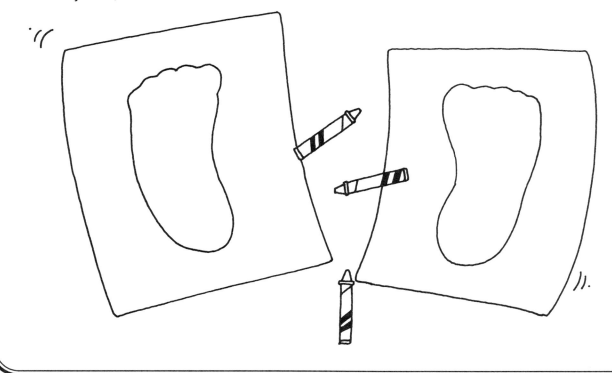

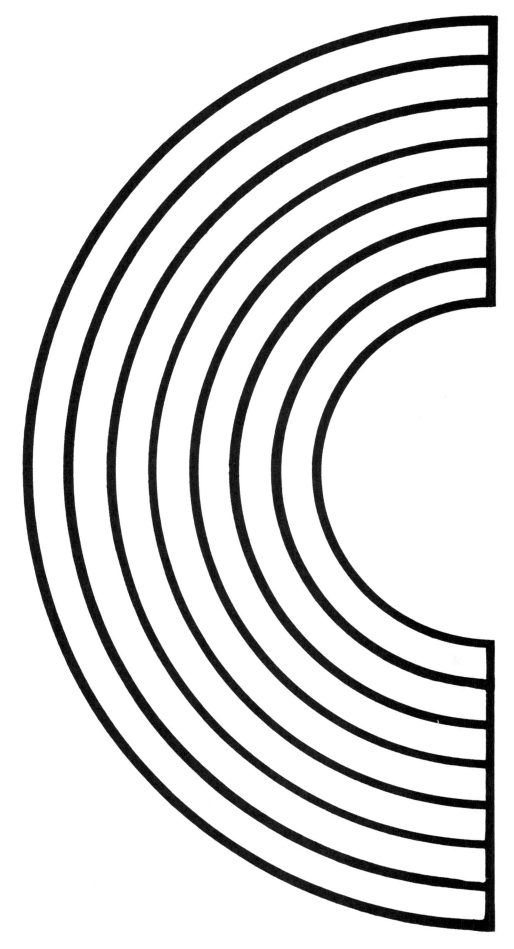

39

SS3825

40

Materials:

background paper, scissors, stapler, black marker, 5" x 9" index card, large manila envelope, construction paper (variety including dark brown, light brown, and gray), pencil

Directions:

1. Cover the board with background paper. Cut letters for the caption from construction paper (any color).
2. Enlarge the basket pattern on page 43. Trace and cut four baskets from dark brown construction paper. On each basket, print one of the following reference tools:
   Atlas   Concordance   Commentary   Bible Dictionary
   Attach the baskets to the board, leaving the tops open.
3. Reproduce the fish pattern on page 44. Trace and cut eight fish from gray construction paper. On each fish, write one of the following numbers and questions:
   1. the location of the Red Sea 3. a map of Paul's missionary journeys 5. the meaning of the word "covenant" 7. how to spell the word "prodigal" 9. where to find the word "fish" in the Bible 11. someone else's ideas of what the Bible means 13. what the Book of Revelation means 15. how many times the word "bread" is found in the Bible
4. Reproduce the loaf pattern on page 44. Trace and cut eight loaves from light brown construction paper. On each loaf, write one of the following numbers and questions:
   2. how to pronounce the word "Gilead" 4. whether the word "Abba" is a noun or a verb 6. where the town of Bethlehem is 8. where the wall of Jericho was 10. a verse in the Bible that has the word "loaves" in it 12. a verse in the Bible about being "fishers of men" 14. the meaning of some of the Parables of Jesus 16. the meaning of some of the Hebrew customs of the Old Testament
5. Print the following directions on the 5" x 9" card:
   Reference books such as the atlas, dictionary, commentary, and concordance can help

us understand the Bible better. An atlas is a book of maps showing where places are. A dictionary tells us about words. A commentary is another person's ideas about something in the Bible, and a concordance lists places to find certain words in the Bible. Each type of reference is written on a basket. Read each fish and loaf. Decide which reference tool you would use to find the information. Put the fish or loaf in that basket. (Check your answers by looking on the back of this card.)

On the back of the card write this answer key:

Atlas–1, 3, 6, 8 Concordance–9, 10, 12, 15 Commentary–11, 13, 14, 16 Dictionary–2, 4, 5, 7

6. Write "Where would you find . . . ?" on the front of the envelope. Store fish and loaves in the envelope and secure it to the board.

Follow-Up:

Play Fish 'n' Loaves Reference Relay. Divide the class into two teams (the Fish and the Loaves) and have each team form a line. Devise a list of questions similar to the ones used on the board. Ask the first person in each line a question. Whoever says the correct reference tool gets a point for that team. After each question, the first person in line moves to the back so everyone can have a turn.

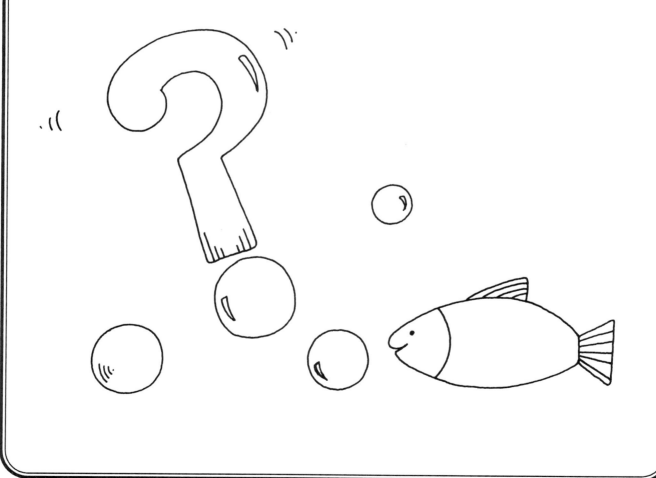

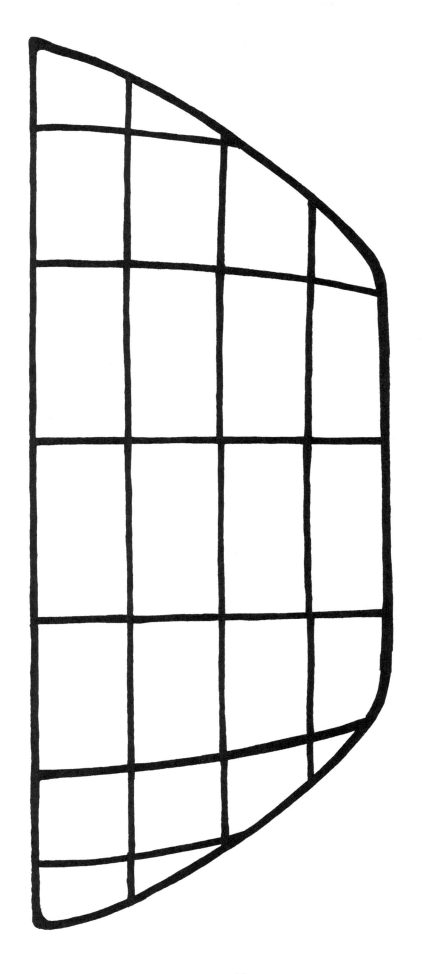

SS3825

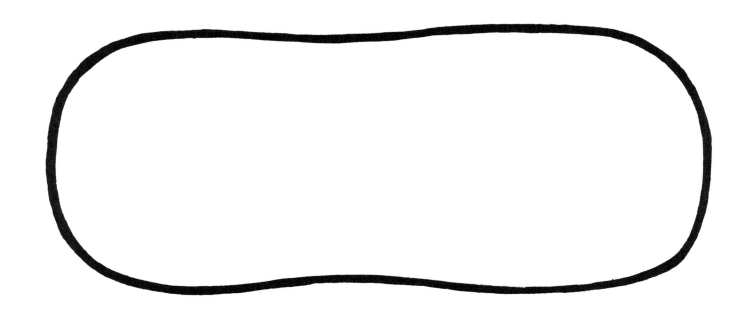

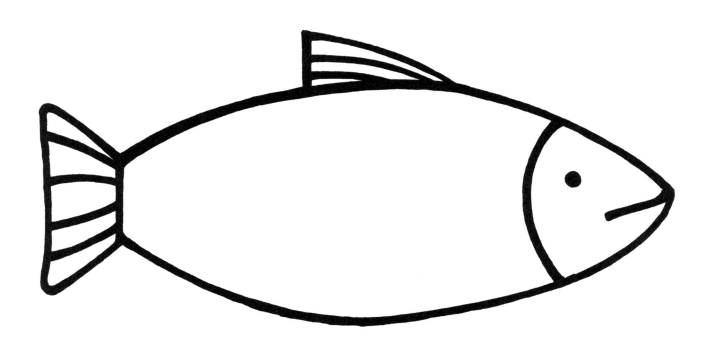

44

Materials:

blue background paper, black marker, stapler, scissors, construction paper (all colors), Velcro™, 5" x 9" index card, large plastic storage bag, pencil, pushpins

Directions:

1. Cover the board with background paper. Cut letters for the caption from construction paper.
2. Reproduce the branch, leaf, and cocoon patterns on page 47. Trace and cut from construction paper five brown branches, five green leaves, and five gray cocoons. On each cocoon, write one of the following numbers, verses, and references:
   1. "They divide my garments among them and cast lots for my clothing." Psalm 22:18
   2. "But you, Bethlehem Ephrathah, though you are small among the clans of Judah, out of you will come for me one who will be ruler over Israel, whose origins are from of old, from ancient times." Micah 5:2
   3. "Therefore the Lord himself will give you a sign: The virgin will be with child and will give birth to a son . . . ." Isaiah 7:14
   4. "See, your king comes to you, righteous and having salvation, gentle and riding on a donkey, on a colt, the foal of a donkey." Zechariah 9:9b
   5. "But God will redeem my life from the grave; he will surely take me to himself." Psalm 49:15

Attach the branches, leaves, and cocoons to the board as shown. Attach a small piece of Velcro™ near each cocoon.

3. Reproduce the butterfly on page 48. Trace and cut from colored construction paper five butterflies. On each butterfly write one of the following verses and references:
   - "When they had crucified him, they divided up his clothes by casting lots." Matthew 27:35
   - "After Jesus was born in Bethlehem in Judea, during the time of King Herod . . . ." Matthew 2:1-2
   - "When they brought the colt to Jesus and threw their cloaks over it, he sat on it." Mark 11:7
   - "The virgin's name was Mary. The angel went to her and said, 'Greetings, you who are highly favored! The Lord is with you. You will be with child and give birth to a son, and you are to give him the name Jesus.'" Luke 1:27b-28, 31
   - "'Don't be alarmed,' he said. 'You are looking for Jesus the Nazarene, who was crucified. He has risen! He is not here.'" Mark 16:6a

   Fold each butterfly slightly in half, bending the wings. Attach a piece of Velcro™ to the back of each butterfly at the fold line.

4. Write these directions on the 5" x 9" card:

   Some parts of the Old Testament tell about something that will happen in the future—a prophecy. Many of these prophecies are about the coming Messiah, Jesus! Read the Old Testament prophecy on each cocoon. Take out the butterflies in this bag and read on them how these prophecies were fulfilled in the New Testament. Try to match each cocoon with the butterfly that tells how Jesus answered, or fulfilled, that prophecy. Use your Bible for help. (Check your answers by turning this card over.)

   On the back of the card write this answer key:

   1. Matthew 27:35; 2. Matthew 2:1-2; 3. Luke 1:27b-28, 31; 4. Mark 11:7; 5. Mark 16:6a

5. Store the directions card and butterflies in the plastic storage bag and secure it to the board with pushpins.

Follow-Up:

Explore some of the prophecies concerning the second coming of Jesus (such as Matthew 24; Mark 13; Luke 21; 1 Thessalonians 4; and 2 Thessalonians 2). Have students glue four construction paper circles (approximately 2" in diameter) together to form a caterpillar. Add eyes, mouth, and pipe cleaner antennae, and finish by writing "Jesus Is Coming Soon!" on the circles.

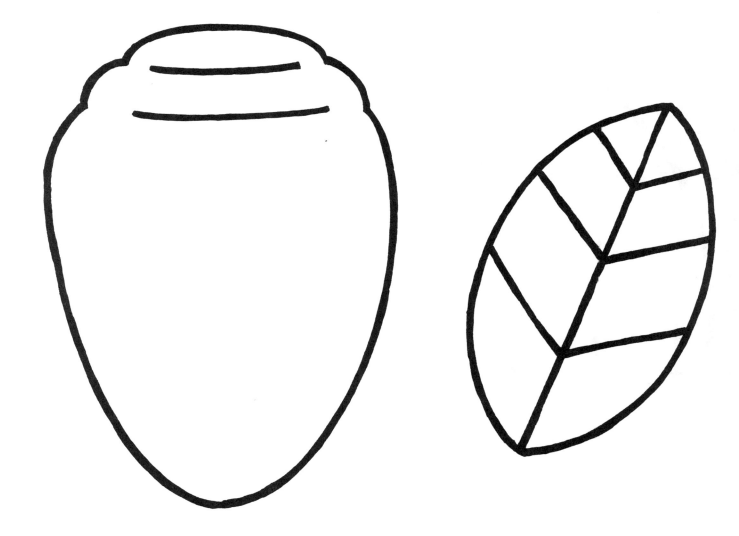

SS3825

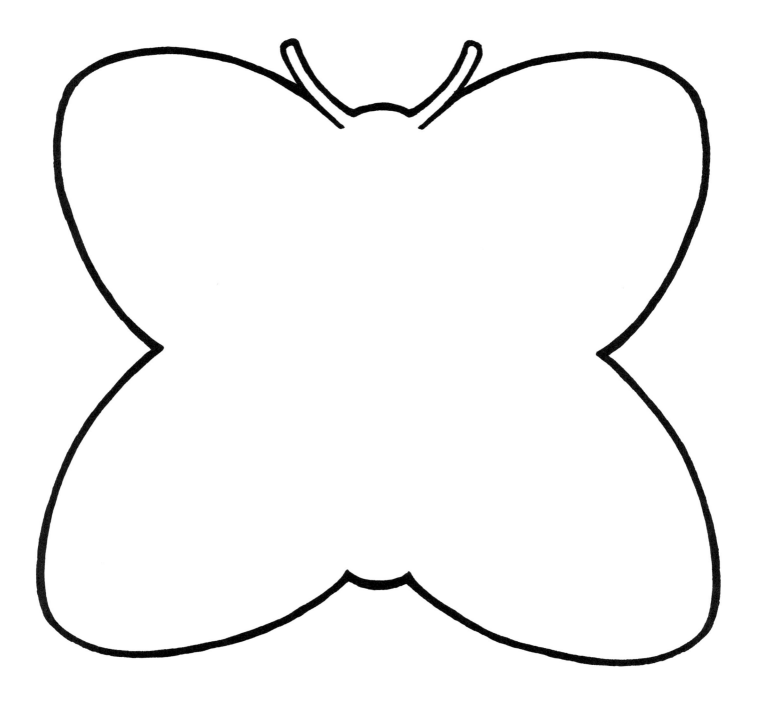

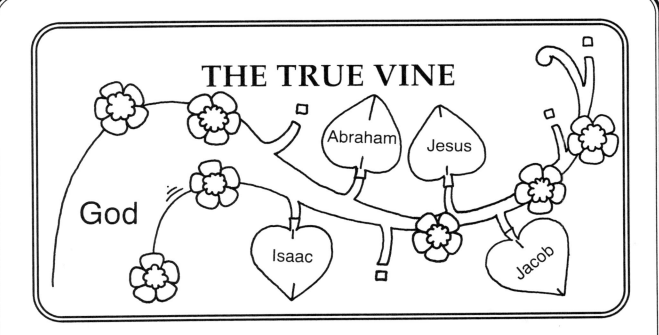

THE TRUE VINE

God

Abraham

Jesus

Isaac

Jacob

Materials:

blue background paper, scissors, stapler, brown poster paint, Velcro™ , glue, construction paper (green, black, pink, yellow), plastic storage bag, tissue paper, 5" x 9" index card, pushpins, pencil, black marker

Directions:

1. Cover the board with background paper and cut letters for the caption from pink construction paper.
2. Using brown poster paint, draw a large stem and trailing vine as shown. Place small pieces of Velcro™ at eight different places along the vine.
3. Cut letters for "God" from black construction paper and staple them to the stem.
4. Reproduce the flower on page 50. Trace and cut several flowers from pink construction paper (use balled-up tissue paper for flower centers) and staple them to the vine.
5. Reproduce the leaf, page 50. Trace and cut eight leaves from green construction paper. On each leaf write one of the following names:
   Adam   Noah   Abraham   Isaac   Jacob   David   Solomon   Jesus
   Place a small piece of Velcro™ on the back of each leaf.
6. On the 5" x 9" card, write the following directions:
   Did you know that Jesus was descended from some famous people in the Bible? Look up Luke 3:23-38 and Matthew 1:1-17. These listings of Jesus' family history are called genealogies. Each leaf in this bag has the name of one of Jesus' ancestors on it (including Jesus). Using the genealogies, see if you can put the leaves in order on the vine. Two names are not included in the genealogies. (Check your answers by looking on the back of this card when you are done.)
   On the back of the card write this answer key (Keep the names in this order.):
   Adam   Noah   Abraham   Isaac   Jacob   David   Solomon   Jesus
7. Store the directions card and leaves in the plastic bag. Attach it to the board with pushpins.

Follow-Up:

Have students use construction paper vines and leaves to construct their own "family vines."

SS3825

50

SS3825

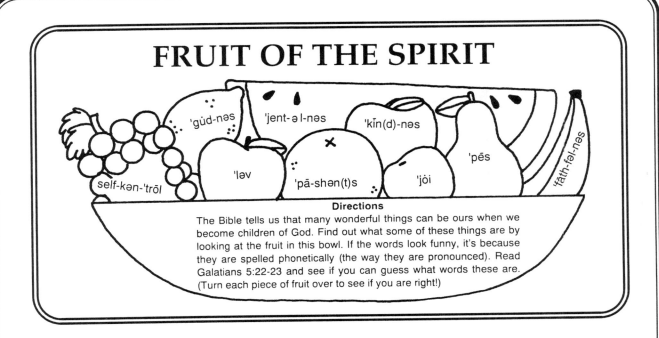

FRUIT OF THE SPIRIT

Directions

The Bible tells us that many wonderful things can be ours when we become children of God. Find out what some of these things are by looking at the fruit in this bowl. If the words look funny, it's because they are spelled phonetically (the way they are pronounced). Read Galatians 5:22-23 and see if you can guess what words these are. (Turn each piece of fruit over to see if you are right!)

Materials:

background paper (a light color), construction paper (black and brown), markers (including black), scissors, stapler

Directions:

1. Cover the board with background paper and cut letters for the caption from black construction paper. Attach them to the board as shown.
2. Cut a fruit bowl shape from brown construction paper. Print these directions on the bowl:
   The Bible tells us that many wonderful things can be ours when we become children of God. Find out what some of these things are by looking at the fruit in this bowl. If the words look funny, it's because they are spelled phonetically (the way they are pronounced). Read Galatians 5:22-23 and see if you can guess what words these are. (Turn each piece of fruit over to see if you are right!)
3. Reproduce, color, and cut out each fruit on pages 52-56. On the back of each fruit write the correct answer:
   Apple–Love, Orange–Patience, Banana–Faithfulness, Plum–Joy, Peach–Kindness, Watermelon–Gentleness, Lemon–Goodness, Pear–Peace, Grapes–Self-Control
4. Arrange the fruit in the bowl.

Follow-Up:

For a special treat, assign each student to bring a different fruit to class. Peel and chop your way to a "Fruit of the Spirit" fruit salad!

  SS3825

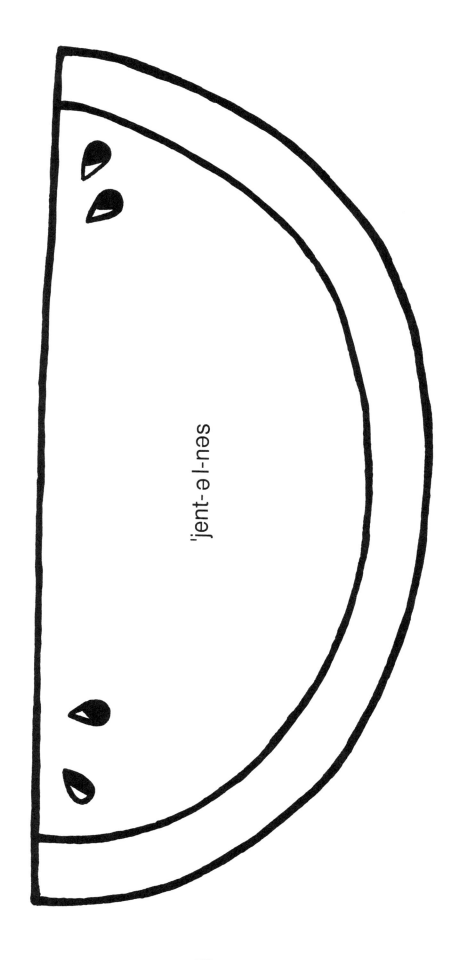

'jent-e-lun,

52

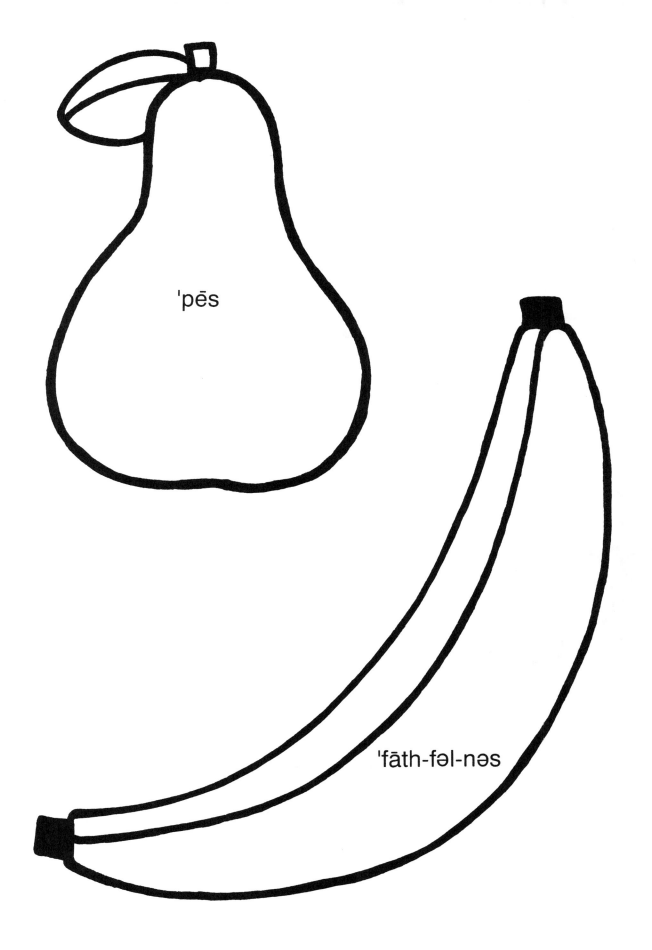

'pēs

'fāth-fəl-nəs

53

SS3825

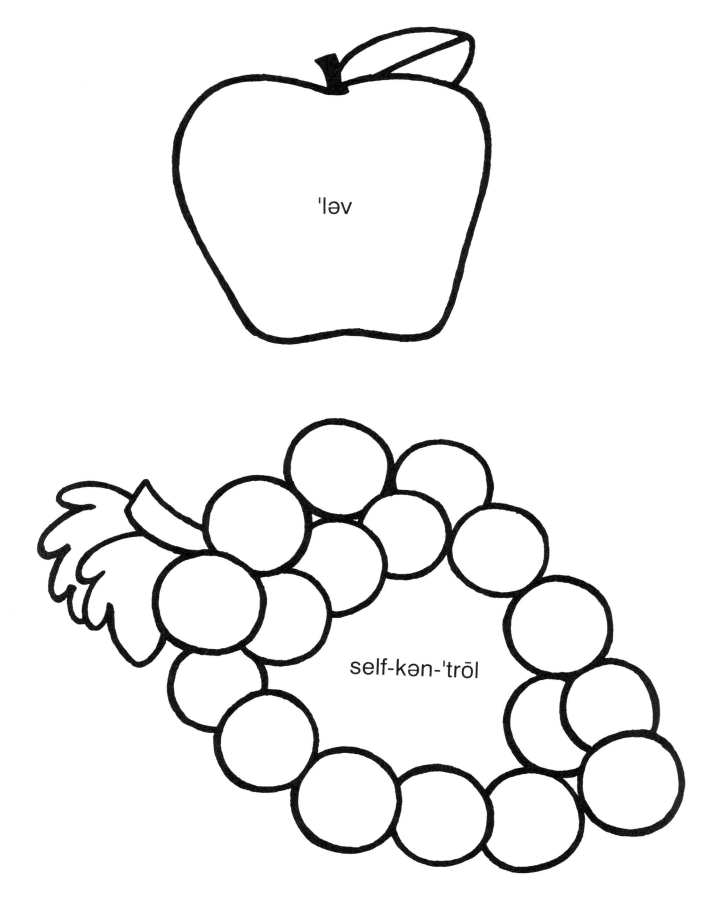

'ləv

self-kən-'trōl

54

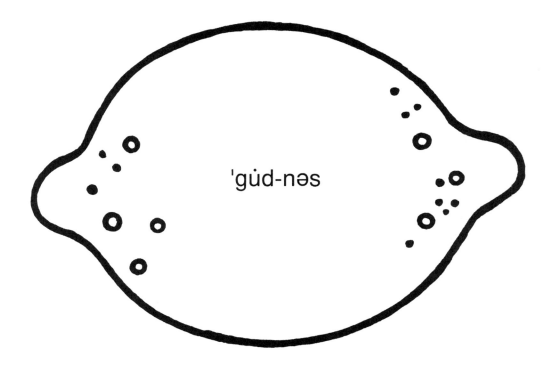

'gu̇d-nəs

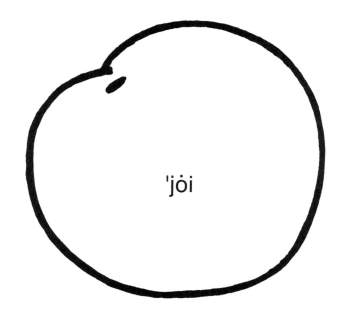

'jȯi

SS3825

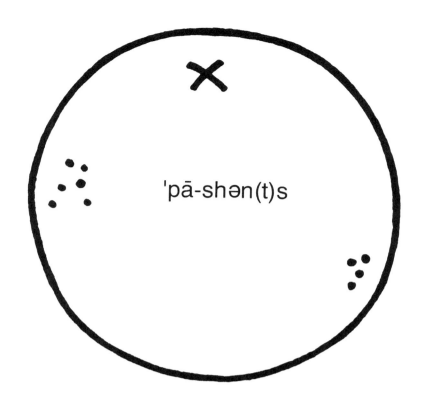

'pā-shən(t)s

'kīn(d)-nəs

56

SS3825

BIBLICAL COINS

Materials:

blue background paper, scissors, stapler, markers (including black), construction paper (variety including green), pencil, large plastic storage bag, pushpins

Directions:

1. Cover the board with background paper. Cut letters for the caption from construction paper (any color).
2. Enlarge the fish on page 59. Trace and cut six fish from green construction paper. On five of the fish, write the following references:
   Ezra 2:69; Exodus 38:28; Matthew 5:25-26; Matthew 25:14-15; Matthew 20:1-2
   On the sixth fish, write these directions:
   In Matthew 17:24-27, Jesus tells Peter to catch a fish with a coin in its mouth! What types of coins does the Bible mention? Look up the verses on these fish. Find the coins mentioned in the verses and put them in the fish's mouths. (To check your answers, look on the back of this fish's coin.)
   Attach the fish to the board as shown.
3. Reproduce, color, and cut out the coins on page 58. Make the denarius and drachma silver, the penny and shekel brown, and the talent gold. On the back of the answer coin write this answer key. Ezra 2:69—drachma, Exodus 38:28—shekel, Matthew 5:25-26—penny, Matthew 25:14-15—talent, Matthew 20:1-2—denarius. Place the answer coin in the mouth of the directions fish and the other coins in the plastic storage bag, and secure it to the board with pushpins.

Follow-Up:

Assign common monetary values to each coin (example: a talent is a dollar, a drachma becomes a quarter, a denarius a dime, a shekel a nickle, and a penny a penny) and devise simple math problems for the students to solve.

talent

denarius

drachma

Answers

shekel

penny

SS3825

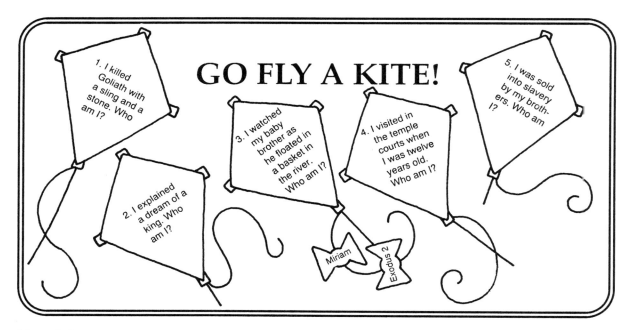

GO FLY A KITE!

1. I killed Goliath with a sling and a stone. Who am I?

2. I explained a dream of a king. Who am I?

3. I watched my baby brother as he floated in a basket in the river. Who am I?

4. I visited in the temple courts when I was twelve years old. Who am I?

5. I was sold into slavery by my brothers. Who am I?

Miriam

Exodus 2

Materials:

light blue background paper, string, scissors, stapler, construction paper (variety including white), Velcro™ , 5" x 9" index card, plastic storage bag, black marker, pencil, pushpins

Directions:

1. Cover the board with background paper. Cut the caption from white construction paper.
2. Enlarge the kite pattern on page 61. Trace five kites from construction paper. Cut them out and label each with one of the following numbers and descriptions:
   1. I killed Goliath with a sling and a stone. Who am I?
   2. I explained the dream of a king. Who am I?
   3. I watched my baby brother as he floated in a basket in the river. Who am I?
   4. I visited in the temple courts when I was twelve years old. Who am I?
   5. I was sold into slavery by my brothers. Who am I?
   Attach the kites to the board. Staple string to the bottom of each and connect it to the edge of the board. Draw a tail on each kite. Place two pieces of Velcro™ on the tail.
3. Use the bow pattern on page 61 to trace and cut ten bows from construction paper. Divide the bows into pairs. On each pair write one of these names and references: David/1 Samuel 17:48-50; Daniel/Daniel 2; Moses' sister Miriam/Exodus 2; Jesus/Luke 2:41-52; Joseph/Genesis 37:12-36. Attach a piece of Velcro™ to the back of each bow.
4. Write these directions on the 5" x 9" card:
   Did you know that there are many stories about kids in the Bible? Read each kite for a description of a "King's Kid." Take the kite tail "bows" from the bag. Look up the verses on the bows and match the name on each bow with the description on a kite. Put the bows on the correct kites. (Check your answers by looking on the back of this card)
   On the back of the card write this answer key:
   1. David   2. Daniel   3. Miriam   4. Jesus   5. Joseph
5. Store the directions and bows in a plastic storage bag. Secure it to the board with pushpins.

Follow-Up:

Make a copy of the kite pattern for each student to color, cut out, and write his name on. Add these "King's Kids' Kites" to the edge of the board for a colorful border.

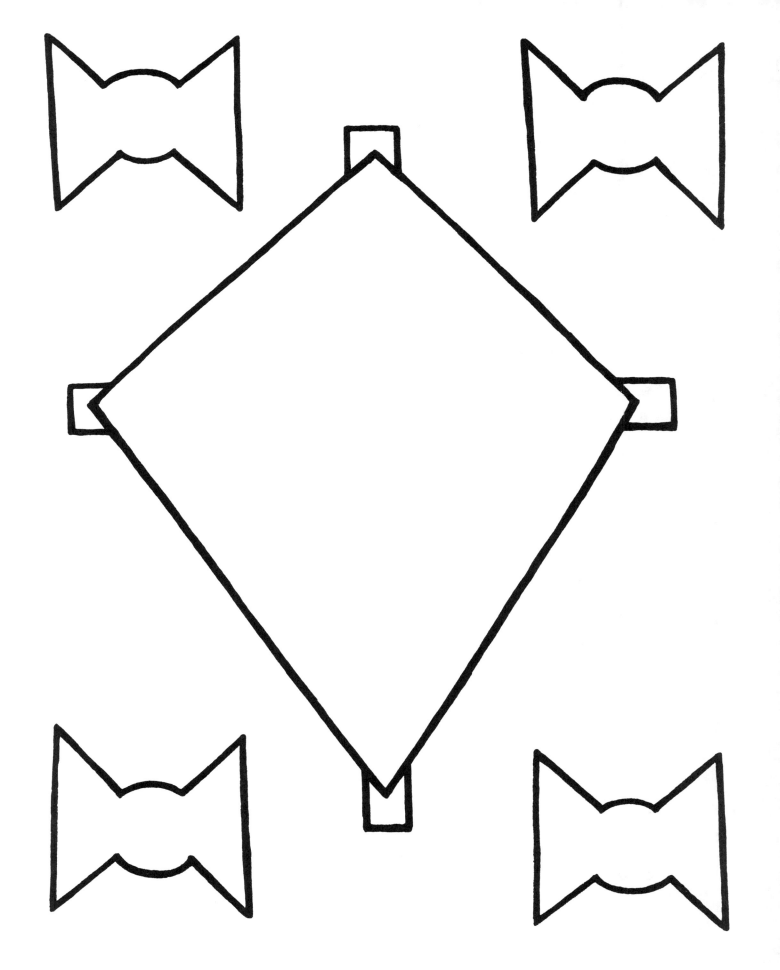

SS3825

Materials:

baby gift wrap, construction paper (pastel colors), markers (including black), scissors, stapler, glue, 5" x 9" index card, plastic storage bag, pencil, pushpins

Directions:

1. Use baby gift wrap for background paper. Cut letters for the caption from pastel-colored construction paper.
2. Reproduce the baby patterns on pages 63-64. Trace and cut out five buntings from pastel construction paper. Reproduce, trace, and cut out the baby heads and hands. Glue them to the bunting as shown, leaving "finger" parts of the hands unglued. Print one of the following numbers, statements, and references on each bunting:
   1. I was found floating in a basket on the Nile. Pharaoh's daughter adopted me. Who am I? (Exodus 2)
   2. I was born holding the heel of my twin brother Esau. Who am I? (Genesis 25:25-26)
   3. I jumped in my mother's womb when I heard the voice of Mary. Who am I? (Luke 1:39-66)
   4. I was born in a stable and visited by shepherds. Who am I? (Luke 2:8-21)
   5. My mother promised I would serve the Lord always. Who am I? (1 Samuel 1:11-20)
   Staple the babies to the board as shown.
3. Reproduce, color, and cut out the toys on pages 64-66. Print these corresponding numbers on the backs of the toys:
   Duck–1   Teddy Bear–2   Rattle–3   Bottle–4   Pacifier–5
4. On the 5" x 9" card write these directions:
   Can you guess the names of these famous Bible babies? Read the description on each baby; then try to match it with the toy with the correct name on it (put the toy in the baby's hand). To check your answers, look on the back of each toy!
5. Store the directions card and toy pictures in a storage bag and secure it to the board with pushpins.

Follow-Up:

Invite students to create "birth announcements" for Bible babies. Be sure they include each baby's name and imagined birth weight and height.

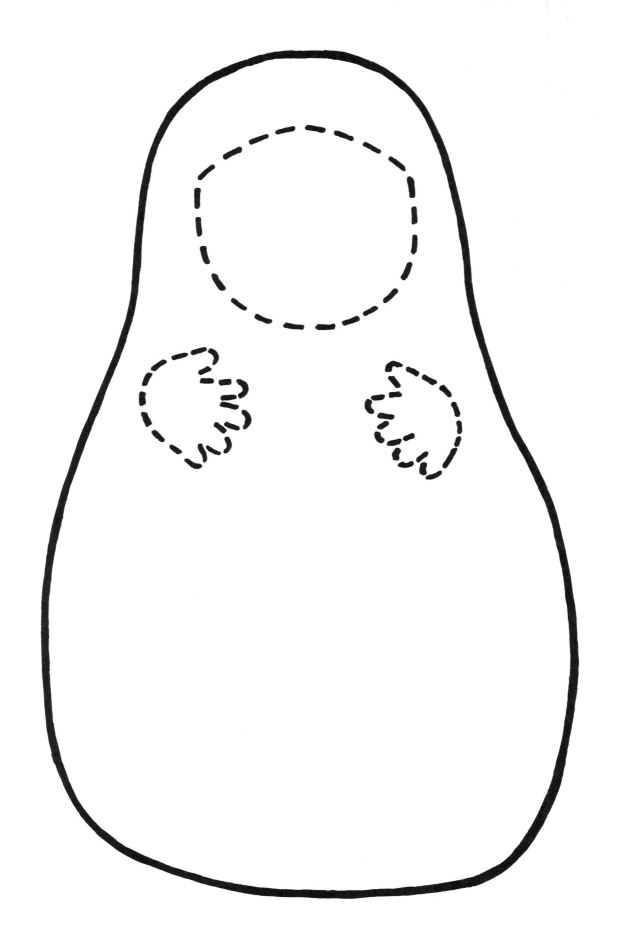

SS3825

Jacob

64

SS3825

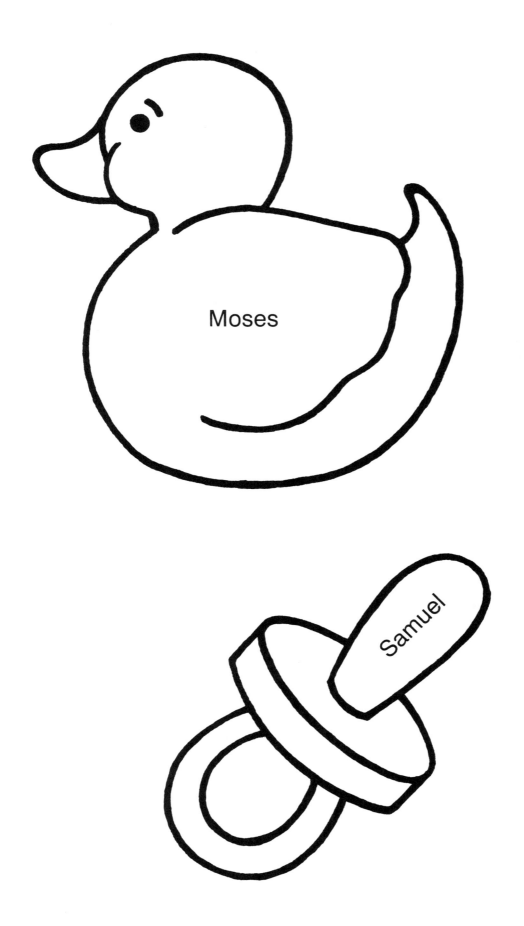

Moses

Samuel

SS3825

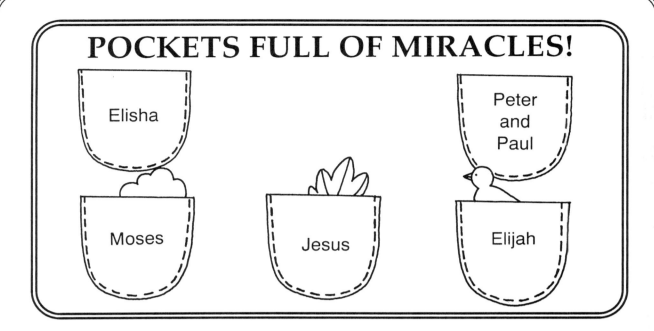

POCKETS FULL OF MIRACLES!

Materials:

background paper (any color), markers (including black), stapler, scissors, construction paper (all colors), 5" x 9" index card, large manila envelope, pencil

Directions:

1. Cover the board with background paper and cut letters for the caption from construction paper.
2. Reproduce the pocket on page 68. Trace and cut out five pockets from different colors of construction paper. On each pocket write one of the following names:
   Moses   Jesus   Elisha   Elijah   Peter and Paul
   Attach pockets to the board as shown, leaving the top of each pocket open.
3. Reproduce, color, and cut out the miracle symbols on pages 69-74. On the back of each picture, write the corresponding answer:
   Staff, stone, and cloud–Moses   Water drop, oil jar, and ax–Elisha
   Bread, fig leaf, and wave–Jesus   Shadow and gate–Peter
   Umbrella, fire, and raven–Elijah   Prison bars and snake–Paul
4. Write these directions on the 5" x 9" card:
   A miracle is something God makes happen. It is so special, no one can explain it! Each pocket on the board has the name of someone in the Bible who was able to perform the miracles of God. Read each miracle symbol in this envelope. Use your Bible to look up the verses and find out who performed each miracle. Put the symbol in that person's pocket. (To check your answers turn each picture over.)
5. Write "Who did it?" on the front of the manila envelope. Store the directions card and miracle symbols in the envelope and attach it to the board.

Follow-Up:

Have each student cut two matching pocket shapes from construction paper. Punch holes in three of the sides, leaving the tops open.Thread yarn through the holes, tying off at each end. Talk about how God responds to the requests of His people. Encourage students to write their prayer requests on slips of paper and keep them in their "Prayer Pockets."

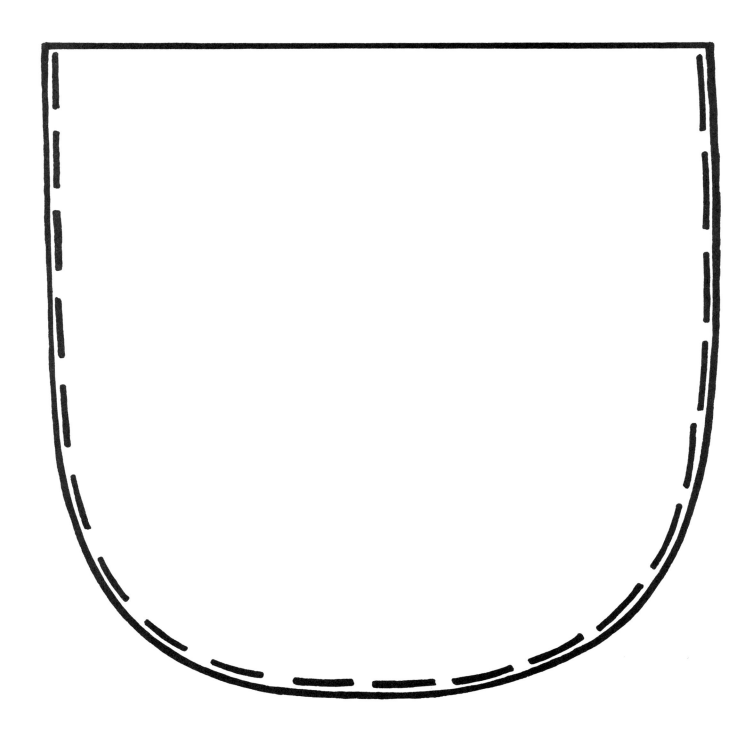

SS3825

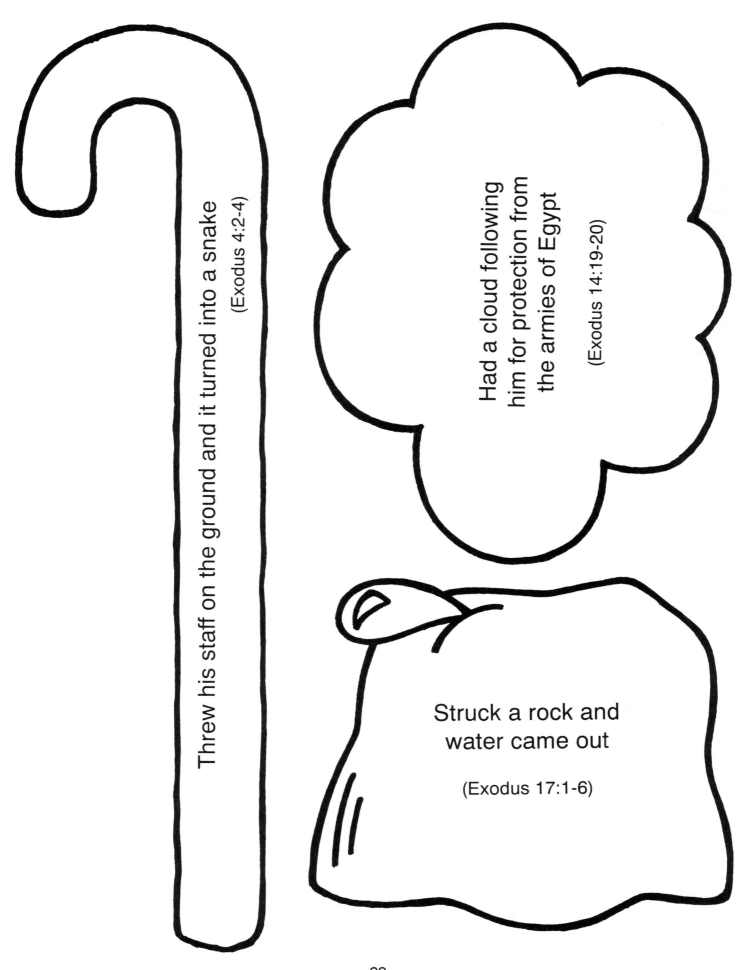

Threw his staff on the ground and it turned into a snake (Exodus 4:2-4)

Had a cloud following him for protection from the armies of Egypt (Exodus 14:19-20)

Struck a rock and water came out

(Exodus 17:1-6)

SS3825

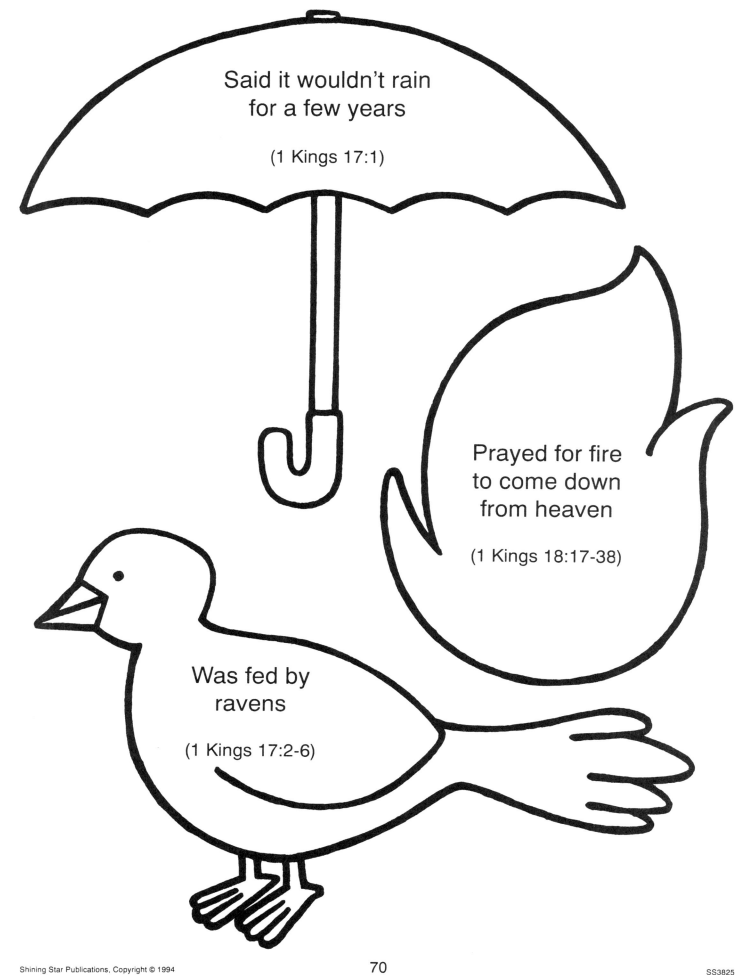

Said it wouldn't rain for a few years

(1 Kings 17:1)

Prayed for fire to come down from heaven

(1 Kings 18:17-38)

Was fed by ravens

(1 Kings 17:2-6)

70

SS3825

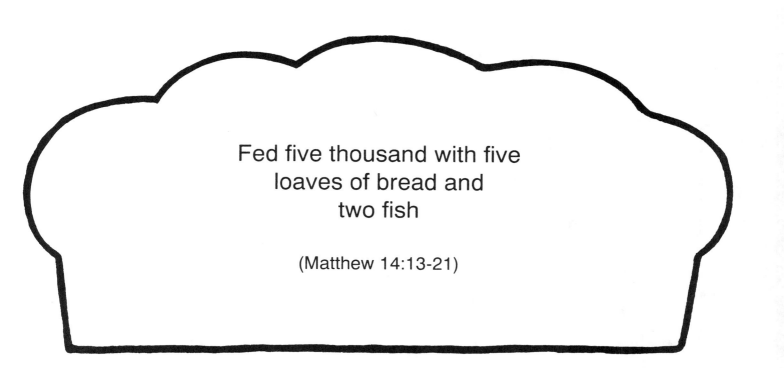

Fed five thousand with five
loaves of bread and
two fish

(Matthew 14:13-21)

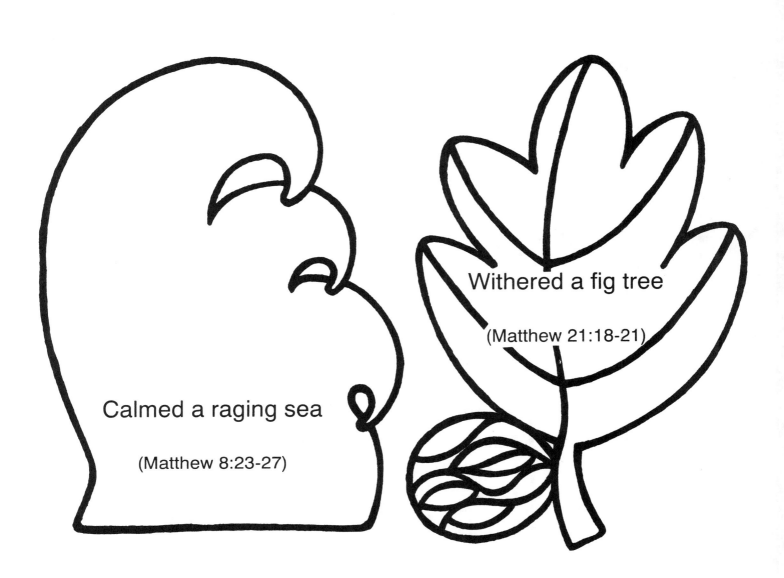

Withered a fig tree

(Matthew 21:18-21)

Calmed a raging sea

(Matthew 8:23-27)

SS3825

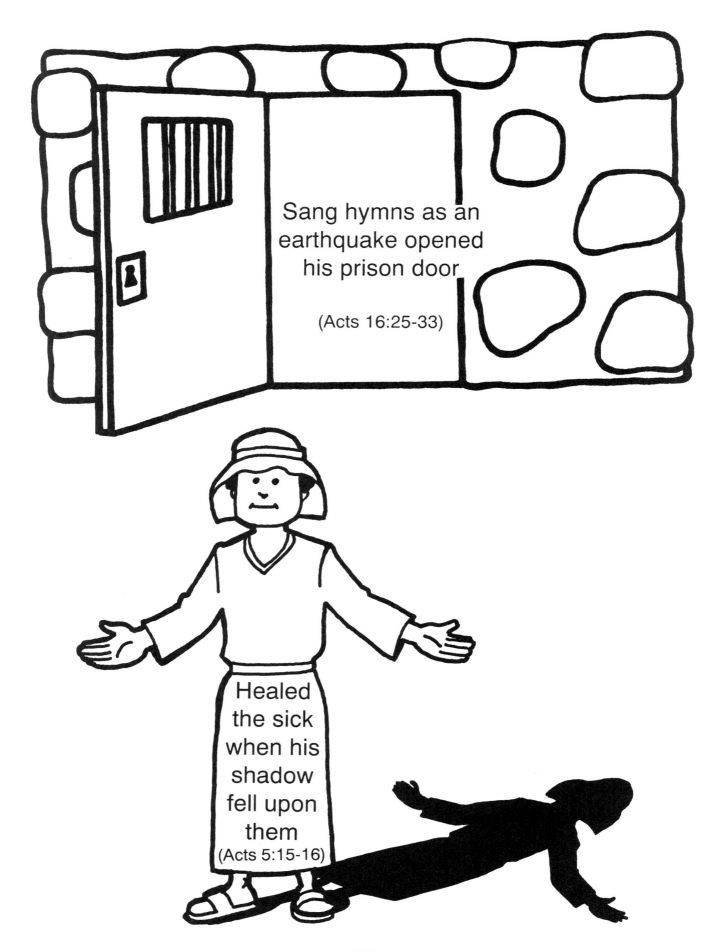

Sang hymns as an earthquake opened his prison door

(Acts 16:25-33)

Healed the sick when his shadow fell upon them

(Acts 5:15-16)

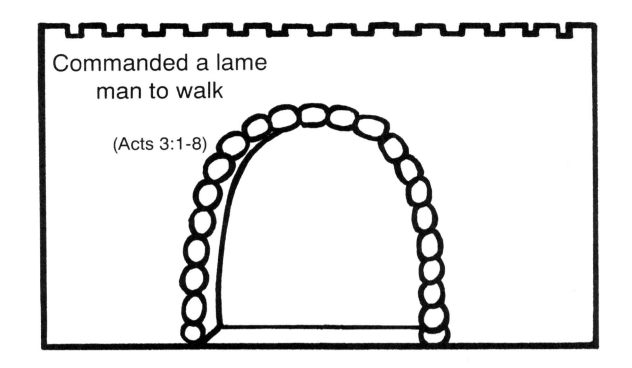

Commanded a lame
man to walk

(Acts 3:1-8)

Was bitten by a poisonous snake but wasn't hurt

(Acts 28:3-6)

SS3825

Made an
axhead
float in
water

(2 Kings 6:4-7)

Made a widow's jar
give lots of oil

(2 Kings 4:1-7)

Filled the land
with water

(2 Kings 3:14-20)

SS3825

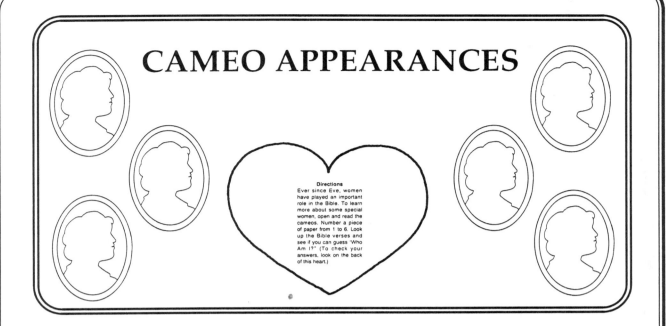

Materials:

background paper (light color), scissors, glue, black marker, stapler, pushpins, construction paper (pastel colors, ivory, and black), pencil

Directions:

1. Cover the board with background paper and cut letters for the caption from construction paper.
2. Using the patterns on page 77, reproduce, trace, and cut out six cameo patterns from ivory construction paper, six small ovals from pastel construction paper, and six large ovals from black construction paper. Glue each cameo to the front of a small oval; then glue the left side to the front of larger oval. Inside each completed cameo, glue one of the "Who Am I?" descriptions on page 78. Staple the backs of the cameos to the board.
3. Reproduce and trace the heart on page 76 from pink construction paper. On the front write these directions:
   Ever since Eve, women have played an important role in the Bible. To learn more about some special women, open and read the cameos. Number a piece of paper from 1 to 6. Look up the Bible verses and see if you can guess "Who Am I?" (To check your answers, look on the back of this heart.)
   On the back of the heart write this answer key:
   1. Deborah; 2. Esther; 3. Sarah; 4. Mary Magdalene; 5. Eve; 6. Mary
   Attach the heart to the board with a pushpin.

Follow-Up:

Using the cameo pattern, ask each student to create a cameo using construction paper, scissors, and glue. Inside, each child should write the description of a Christian woman he knows and admires. The finished cameo may be presented to that person as a special gift.

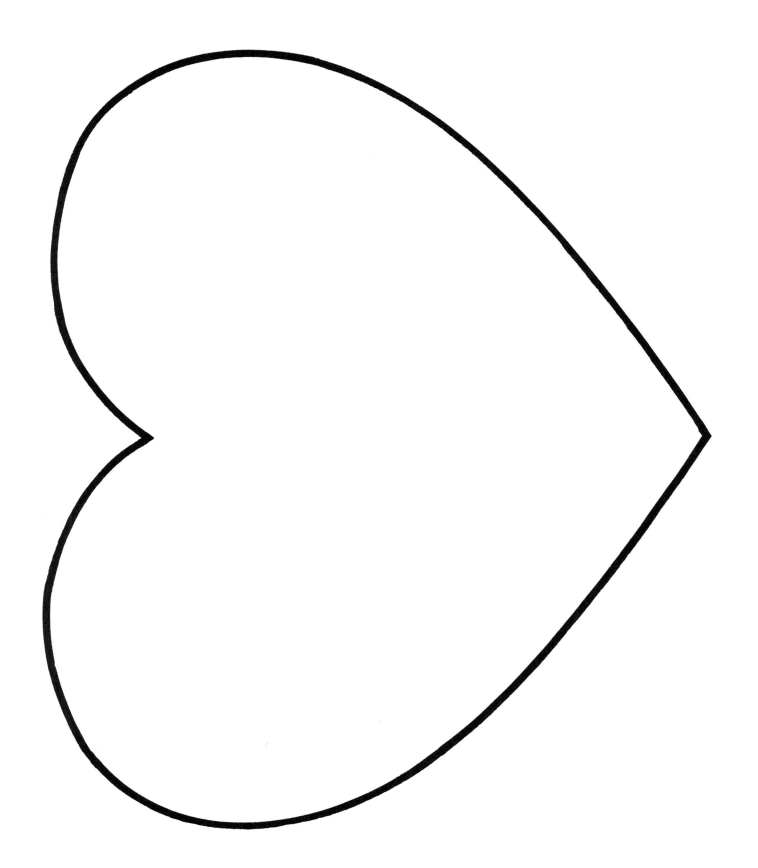

76

SS3825

SS3825

1.
I was a judge in Israel and also a prophetess.
Who am I?

Judges 4:4

2.
I was a queen who helped save my people from destruction.
Who am I?

Esther 4:5

3.
I laughed when the Lord said I would have a child in my old age!
Who am I?

Genesis 18:13-14

4.
I went to Jesus' tomb only to find an angel!
Who am I?

John 20:1

5.
I was made from one of Adam's ribs.
Who am I?

Genesis 2:21–3:20

6.
I gave birth to Jesus.
Who am I?

Luke 2:16

SS3825

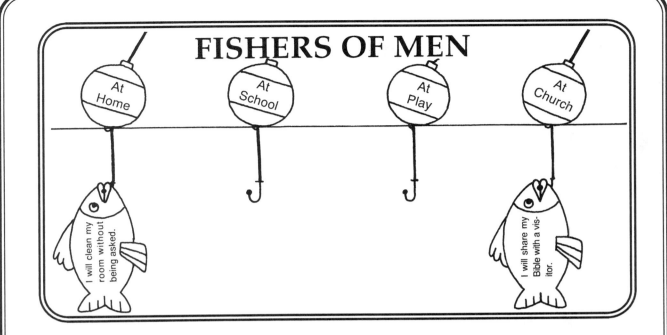

Materials:

background paper (blue, green), string, scissors, stapler, pushpins, markers (including black), construction paper (white), manila envelope, hole punch

Directions:

1. Cover the bottom three-fourths of the board with green background paper. Cover the top one-fourth with blue paper. Cut letters for the caption from white construction paper and attach it to the board.
2. Reproduce the float pattern on page 80. Trace, cut, and color four floats from white construction paper. Write one of the following places on each float:
   At Home   At School   At Church   At Play
   Attach the floats to the board in the order shown.
3. Cut four lengths of string. Staple each to the top of the board, just under the floats and halfway down the green part of the board. With black marker, draw a hook at the end of each string. Place a pushpin at the tip of each hook.
4. Reproduce the fish on page 80. Make one for each student.
5. Write these directions on the front of the manila envelope:
   Jesus called us to be "fishers of men," that is, to lead others to Christ. We can help lead others to Christ by what we say, what we do, and how we treat people. Each of the floats on the board has a special place on it. Think of someone you know at one of these places who may not know Jesus. Think of something you could do to show Jesus to that person. Write on one of the fish what you will do. Keep the fish until you have done what you wrote. Then write your name on the fish, cut it out, punch a hole in its mouth, and put it on the right "hook." See if you can catch a fish on each hook!
6. Store the fish and hole punch in the manila envelope and secure it to the board.

Follow-Up:

Allow students to share their "catches" with the class.

Shining Star Publications, Copyright © 1994   SS3825

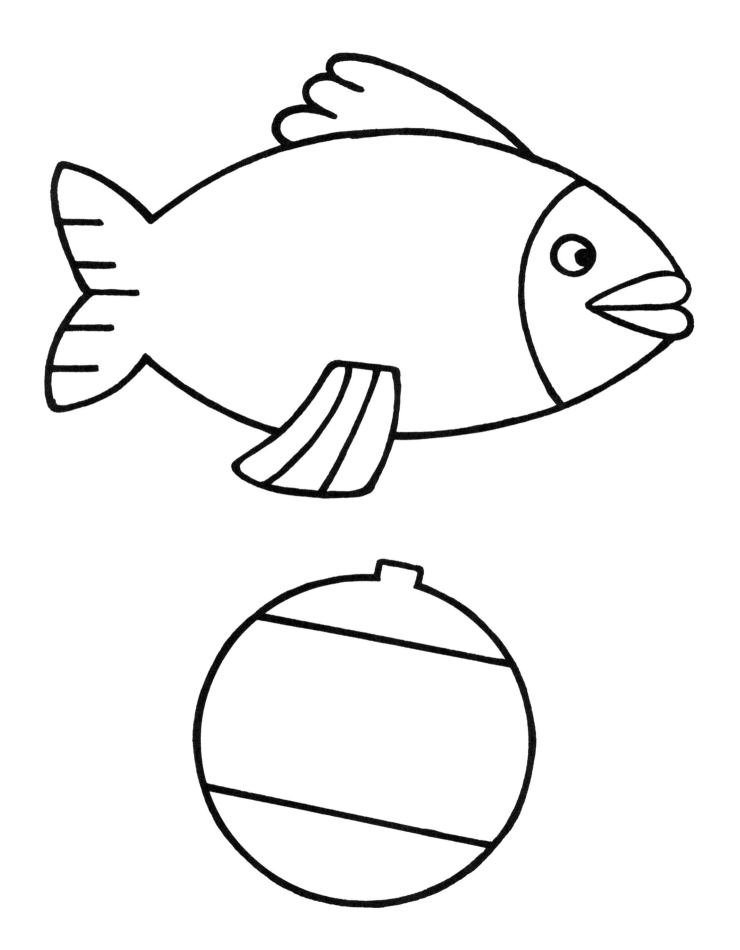

80

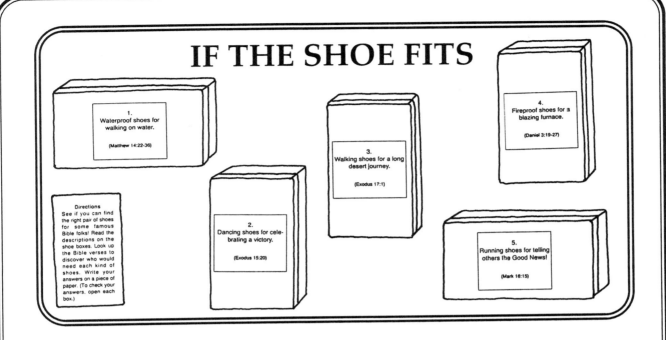

IF THE SHOE FITS

Inside the image:
- 1. Waterproof shoes for walking on water. (Matthew 14:22-36)
- 2. Dancing shoes for celebrating a victory. (Exodus 15:20)
- 3. Walking shoes for a long desert journey. (Exodus 17:1)
- 4. Fireproof shoes for a blazing furnace. (Daniel 3:19-27)
- 5. Running shoes for telling others the Good News! (Mark 16:15)

Directions
See if you can find the right pair of shoes for some famous Bible folks! Read the descriptions on the shoe boxes. Look up the Bible verses to discover who would need each kind of shoes. Write your answers on a piece of paper. (To check your answers, open each box.)

Materials:

background paper (any color), construction paper (white, any color), scissors, stapler, five shoe boxes, glue, black marker, 5" x 9" index card, paper, pencil

Directions:

1. Cover the board with background paper and cut letters for the caption from construction paper.
2. Glue a piece of white construction paper inside each box and write one of the following names on it: Jesus/Peter; Miriam; Israelites; Shadrach, Meshach, and Abednego; You! Staple each box to the board, box top facing out.
3. Reproduce and cut out the description cards on page 82. Glue one card to the top of each shoe box lid. Cover the shoe boxes with the lids that match the description inside: 1–Jesus/Peter, 2–Miriam, 3–Israelites, 4–Shadrach, Meshach, and Abednego, 5–You
4. Write these directions on the 5" x 9" card:
   See if you can find the right pair of shoes for some famous Bible folks! Read the descriptions on the shoe boxes. Look up the Bible verses to discover who would need each kind of shoes. Write your answers on a piece of paper. (To check your answers, open each box.)
5. Staple the directions card to the board.

Follow-Up:

Have students create "fancy footwear" to match the pair of shoes on the board. Place finished, cutout shoes in the correct boxes for other students to admire.

SS3825

1.
Waterproof shoes for walking on water.

(Matthew 14:22-36)

2.
Dancing shoes for celebrating a victory.

(Exodus 15:20)

3.
Walking shoes for a long desert journey.

(Exodus 17:1)

4.
Fireproof shoes for a blazing furnace.

(Daniel 3:19-27)

5.
Running shoes for telling others the Good News!

(Mark 16:15)

SS3825

LIGHTS OF THE WORLD

1. They started a church in their home. (Acts 18:26)
2. She did good and helped the poor. (Acts 9:36-42)
3. She invited missionaries to rest in her home. (Acts 16:13-15)
4. He showed others the truth of the Gospel. (Acts 18:24-28)
5. He gave generously and prayed to God regularly. (Acts 10:2-3)

Materials:

background paper (a dark color), scissors, stapler, Velcro™, black marker, construction paper (white, orange, gold, yellow), pencil, plastic storage bag, pushpins, glue, 5" x 9" index card

Directions:

1. Cover the board with background paper. Cut letters for the caption from yellow construction paper.
2. Reproduce the candle on page 85. Trace and cut five candles from white construction paper. Reproduce the candle holder and make five of them from gold construction paper. On the bottom of each, write one of the following numbers and descriptions:
   1. They started a church in their home. (Acts 18:26)
   2. She did good and helped the poor. (Acts 9:36-42)
   3. She invited missionaries to rest in her home. (Acts 16:13-15)
   4. He showed others the truth of the Gospel. (Acts 18:24-28)
   5. He gave generously and prayed to God regularly. (Acts 10:2-3)
   Attach the candles and candle holders to the board as shown. Use a black marker to draw wicks. Above each wick place a small piece of Velcro™
3. Reproduce the candle flames on page 84. Trace and cut five outer flames from yellow construction paper, and five inner flames from orange construction paper. Glue the inner flames to the outer ones. Write one of these names on each flame:
   Priscilla and Aquila, Dorcas, Lydia, Apollos, Cornelius
   Attach a small piece of Velcro™ to the back of each flame.
4. Print these directions on the 5" x 9" card:
   Read the candles to find out how some Bible people let their lights shine. Match each name with the correct candle. (Check your answers by looking on the back of this card.)
   On the back of the card, write this answer key:
   1. Priscilla and Aquila   2. Dorcas   3. Lydia   4. Apollos   5. Cornelius
5. Store the directions card and flames in a plastic storage bag and secure it to the board with pushpins.

Follow-Up:

Make "Lights of the World" necklaces, using the bulletin board pattern, construction paper, scissors, and glue. Punch a hole in each "flame," thread yarn through it, and knot the ends.

   SS3825

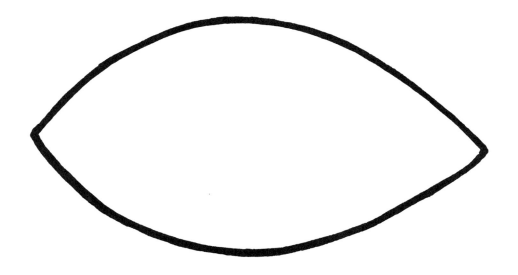

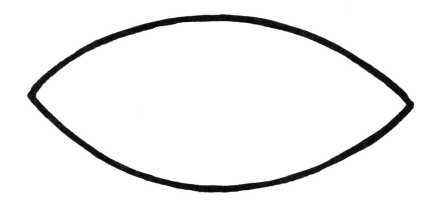

SS3825

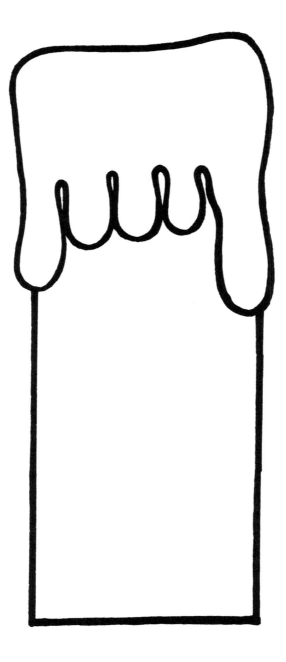

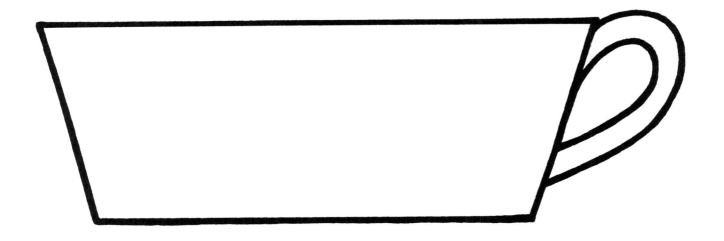

SS3825

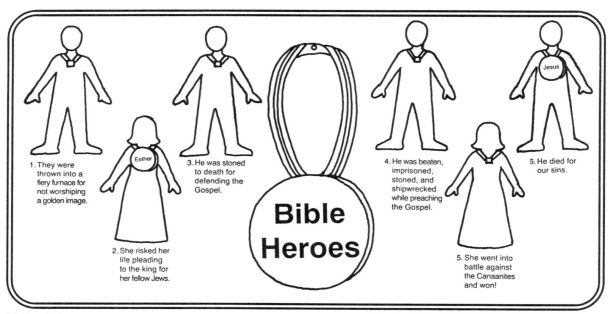

Materials:
background paper (any color), Velcro™, scissors, stapler, 5" x 9" index card, construction paper (variety of colors), plastic storage bag, glue, markers, pencil, ribbon

Directions:
1. Cover the board with background paper. Reproduce, color, and cut out the large medal on page 88. Twist a strip of red construction paper with a white stripe glued to the center, to form the medal's ribbon. Attach it to the center of the board as shown.
2. Reproduce, trace, and cut out four men and two women figures from page 87 from different colors of construction paper. Write a description and number on each:
   WOMEN:
   2. She risked her life pleading to the king for her fellow Jews.
   5. She went into battle against the Canaanites and won!
   MEN:
   1. They were thrown into a fiery furnace for not worshiping a golden image.
   3. He was stoned to death for defending the Gospel.
   4. He was beaten, imprisoned, stoned, and shipwrecked while preaching the Gospel.
   6. He died for our sins.
   Attach each figure to the board, putting a small piece of ribbon around the neck. Place a small piece of Velcro™ where the ribbon comes together at the front of each figure.
3. Reproduce the small medal on page 88. Trace and cut six medals from yellow or gold construction paper. On each one write one of the following names:
   Shadrach, Meshach, and Abednego; Esther; Paul; Deborah; Stephen; Jesus.
   Attach a small piece of Velcro™ to the back of each medal.
4. Write these directions on the 5" x 9" card:
   All Saints' Day is a celebration honoring those who made great sacrifices for their faith. On the board are some Bible heroes. Read the heroes to discover what they did. Read the name on each medal. Match the medal to the correct person. (Check your answers on the back of this card.)
   On the back of the card write this answer key:
   1. Shadrach, Meshach, and Abednego; 2. Esther; 3. Stephen; 4. Paul; 5. Deborah; 6. Jesus.
5. Store the directions card and medals in the plastic storage bag and secure it to the board.

Follow-Up:
Have each student make a hero medal (using the bulletin board pattern, construction paper, and ribbon), and write the name of someone he considers a Christian hero on the medal; then present it to that person.

SS3825

SS3825

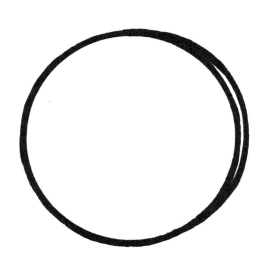

SS3825

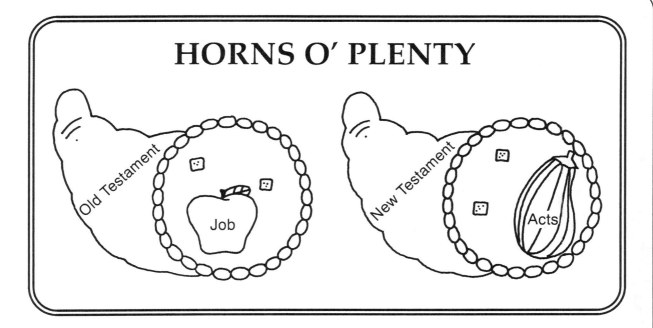

HORNS O' PLENTY

Materials:

background paper (any color), scissors, stapler, black marker, 5" x 9" index card, plastic storage bag, Velcro™, construction paper (variety of colors), pencil, pushpins

Directions:

1. Cover the board with background paper. Cut letters for the caption from construction paper (any color).
2. Enlarge the cornucopia pattern on page 92. Trace and cut two cornucopias from brown construction paper. Write "Old Testament" on one and "New Testament" on the other. Attach them to the board. Determine how many books of the Bible you plan to use, and place a corresponding number of Velcro™ strips on the inside of each cornucopia.
3. Reproduce the fruit, vegetable, and nut patterns on pages 90-91. Cut one for each book of the Bible. Write a different book name on the front of each piece. On the back, attach a piece of Velcro™
4. Write the following directions on the 5" x 9" card:
   Happy Thanksgiving! We have lots to be thankful for when we consider a wonderful gift God has given us–the Bible. Test your Bible knowledge by putting these fruits, vegetables, and nuts in the correct horn o' plenty. (Use your Bible to check your answers.)
5. Store the directions card and food pieces in the plastic storage bag and secure it to the board with pushpins.

Follow-Up:

Have a Horn o' Plenty Spelling Bee on the books of the Bible. Provide each student with a list of books to study beforehand.

SS3825

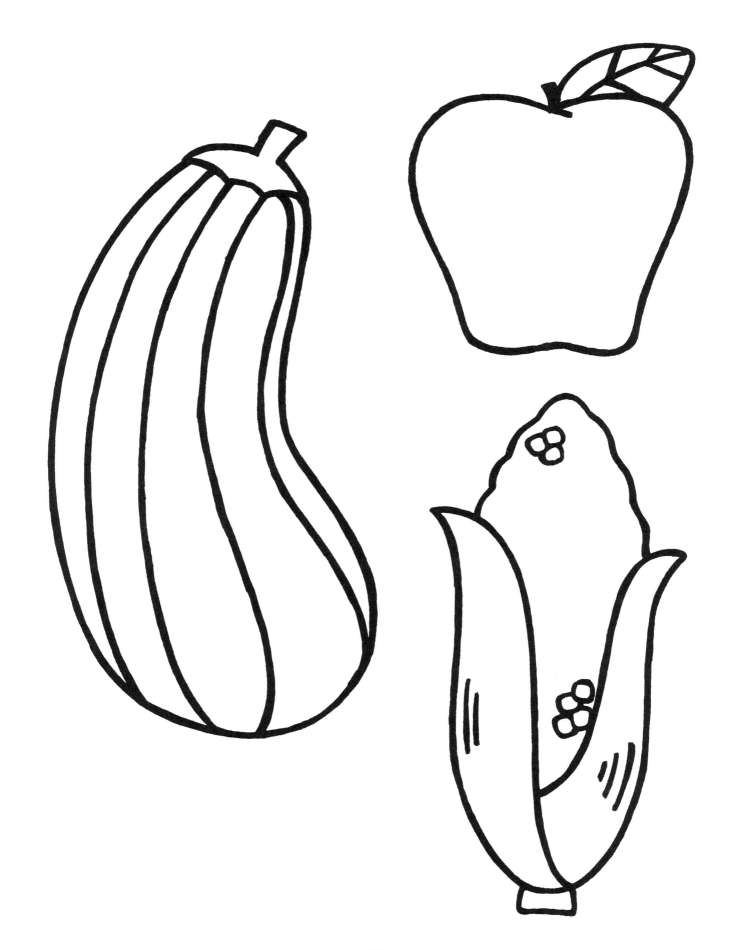

90

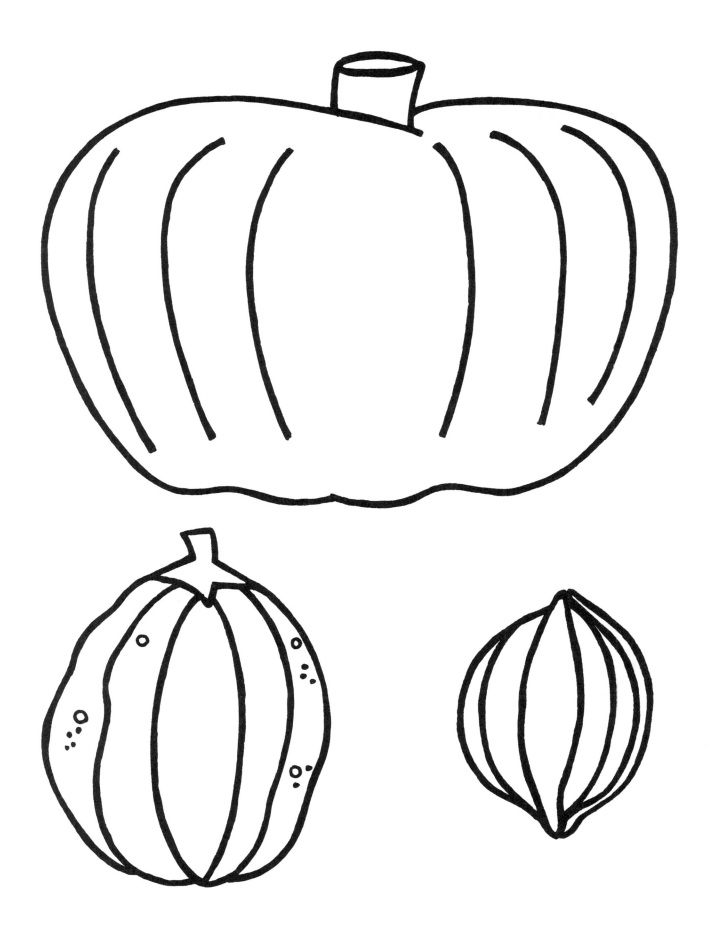

92

SS3825

GIFTS AND GIVERS

1. Jesus (John 3:16)
2. Gold, Spices, and Precious Stones (2 Chronicles 9:1)
3. Coat of Many Colors (Genesis 37:3)
4. Wisdom and Knowledge (1 Corinthians 2)
5. Fattened Calf (Luke 15:23)
6. Gold, Incense, and Myrrh (Matthew 2:11)

Materials:

background paper (any color), wrapping paper, ribbons, scissors, stapler, tape, six gift boxes, construction paper (white), Velcro™, plastic storage bag, black marker, 5" x 9" index card, pushpins

Directions:

1. Cover the board with background paper. Cut letters for the caption from wrapping paper.
2. Staple the bottom of each box to the board.
3. Cover the box lids with wrapping paper. On each lid write one of the following numbers, gifts, and verse references:
   1. Jesus (John 3:16) 2. Gold, Spices, and Precious Stones (2 Chronicles 9:1) 3. Coat of Many Colors (Genesis 37:3) 4. Wisdom and Knowledge (1 Corinthians 2) 5. Fattened Calf (Luke 15:23) 6. Gold, Incense, and Myrrh (Matthew 2:11)
   Decorate the lids with ribbons and slide the lids over the boxes. Place a small piece of Velcro™ on the upper right corner of each box.
4. Reproduce and cut out six gift tags, using the pattern on page 94. Label each tag:
   To: Mankind   To: The Prodigal Son   To: King Solomon
   From: God   From: Father   From: Queen of Sheba
   To: Jesus   To: Joseph   To: Believers in Christ
   From: The Magi (wise men) From: Jacob   From: The Holy Spirit
   Attach a small piece of Velcro™ to the back corner of each tag.
5. Write the following directions on the 5" x 9" card:
   Read the gift tags and use your Bible to decide to whom each gift belongs and who gave it. (Check your answers by looking on the back of this card.)
   On the back of this card write this answer key:
   1. Mankind/God 2. King Solomon/Queen of Sheba 3. Joseph/Jacob 4. Believers in Christ/The Holy Spirit 5. The Prodigal Son/Father 6. Jesus/The Magi
6. Store the directions card and gift tags in a plastic bag and secure it to the board with pushpins.

Follow-Up:

Ask students to think of gifts they have—artistic ability, musical talent, etc. Have them write thank-you notes to God for giving them these gifts. Post the notes on the board.

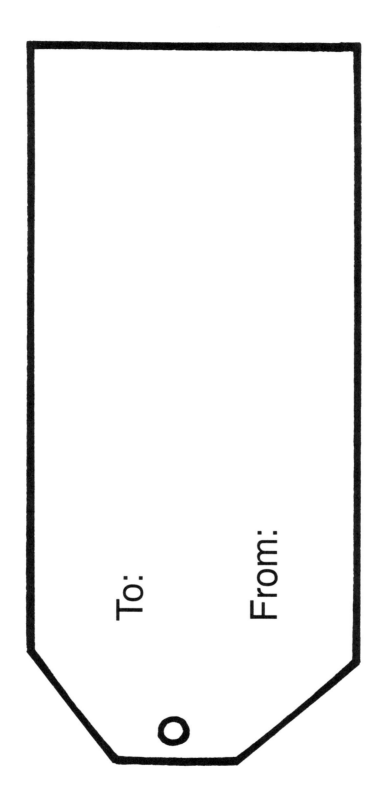

To:

From:

94

SS3825

Materials:

pink background paper, foil (silver or gold), black marker, Velcro™, scissors, stapler, plastic storage bag, 5" x 9" index card, pencil, red construction paper, pushpins

Directions:

1. Cover the board with background paper. Cut letters for the caption from foil.
2. Reproduce the heart on page 96. Trace and cut five hearts from red construction paper. Using a pencil, draw a jagged line down the center of each heart, using a different pattern for each. Using a black marker, write the following couple combinations and verse references on the hearts as shown:
   Adam/Eve (Genesis 3:20), Abraham/Sarah (Genesis 17:15), Isaac/Rebekah (Genesis 25:20), Boaz/Ruth (Ruth 4:13a), Jacob/Rachel (Genesis 29:18)
   Cut the heart in half. Staple half of each heart to the board. Next to each half, place a small piece of Velcro™. Place a small piece of Velcro™ on the back of each remaining half heart also.
3. On the 5" x 9" card, write these directions:
   On Valentine's Day we celebrate love and give heart-shaped valentines. Each of this lesson's "broken" hearts is missing its other half! Read the name on each heart. Using Bible verse references, see if you can match these famous Bible couples. (You will know you have the right match when both sides of the heart fit together!)
4. Store the directions card and heart halves in the plastic storage bag and secure it to the board with pushpins.

Follow-Up:

The Bible has been called "God's letter of love from up above." Have students design valentines and write favorite Bible verses on them. Encourage them to share the valentines with friends.

 SS3825

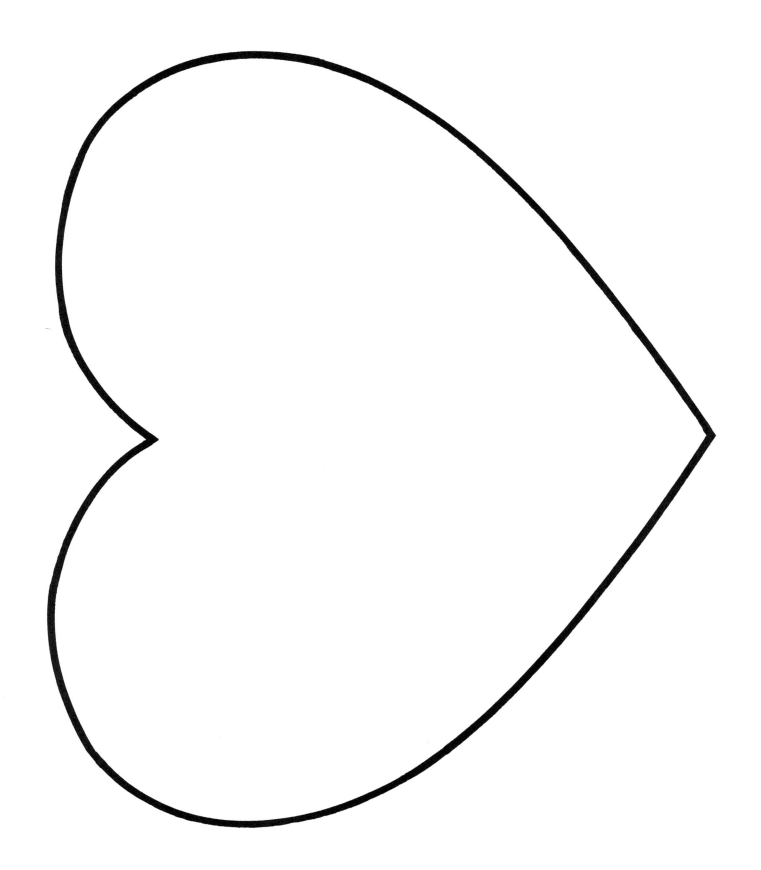

SS3825